Manipu

And

Dark Psychology

2 Books in 1

Protect Yourself from Narcissists and Mind Control. Discover HOW to Analyze People and Boost Emotional Intelligence through a Stoic Way of Life

Daniel Brown

The work contained herein has been produced with the intent to provide relevant knowledge and information on the topic on the topic described in the title for entertainment purposes only. While the author has gone to every extent to furnish up to date and true information, no claims can be made as to its accuracy or validity as the author has made no claims to be an expert on this topic. Notwithstanding, the reader is asked to do their own research and consult any subject matter experts they deem necessary to ensure the quality and accuracy of the material presented herein.

This statement is legally binding as deemed by the Committee of Publishers Association and the American Bar Association for the territory of the United States. Other jurisdictions may apply their own legal statutes. Any reproduction, transmission or copying of this material contained in this work without the express written consent of the copyright holder shall be deemed as a copyright violation as per the current legislation in force on the date of publishing and subsequent time thereafter. All additional works derived from this material may be claimed by the holder of this copyright.

The data, depictions, events, descriptions, and all other information forthwith are considered to be true, fair and accurate unless the work is expressly described as a work of fiction. Regardless of the nature of this work, the Publisher is exempt from any responsibility of actions taken by the reader in conjunction with this work. The Publisher acknowledges that the reader acts of their own accord and releases the author and Publisher of any responsibility for the observance of tips, advice, counsel, strategies, and techniques that may be offered in this volume.

Table of Contents

Dark Psychology

Stoicism

Dark Psychology

The SECRETS Revealed

Protect Yourself from Narcissists, Manipulation, Persuasion, and Mind Control Through an Extreme Crash Course on Body Language, NLP, and Deep Learning

Daniel Brown

accurate unless the work is expressly described as a work of fiction. Regardless of the nature of this work, the Publisher is exempt from any responsibility of actions taken by the reader in conjunction with this work. The Publisher acknowledges that the reader acts of their own accord and releases the author and Publisher of any responsibility for the observance of tips, advice, counsel, strategies, and techniques that may be offered in this volume.

Table of Contents

Chapter 4: Narcissism.......................92

Chapter 5: Understanding Neuro-Linguistic Programming 114

Chapter 6: Hypnosis 129

Introduction

Humans are inherently predictable. Our minds, despite being as complex as they are and despite the intense variation between human behaviors, are incredibly predictable. We can usually influence other people in the same, predictable ways to get the same, predictable results. Especially when people aren't actively guarding against the manipulation that is used. We are easy to control. We are easy to influence. We are easily manipulated.

This fact of life is one that many people have found to be a great asset. All too often, people find that they can use the inherent weaknesses of the human mind to control people—they take charge and make it a point to use people to their advantage. They discover that through using certain behaviors, they can start to influence and control. They learn that, through their actions, they can take charge, to get that complete control over others that gives them what they are trying to get from those around them.

Some people become predators—they become interested in being able to control everything for their selfish purposes. It could be that they feel the need to protect themselves due to being hurt in the past, choosing to manipulate others to get what they need. They go about their lives working to control everyone that they encounter if they can. They want to be able to constantly pull strings from behind the scenes, whether instinctively without thinking about it or because they simply understand people well enough to be able to do so.

Typically, the people who instinctively manipulate others follow very specific patterns that they use to control others. These patterns of behaviors are so predictable that they have been deemed as determinate of dark behaviors. The dark personalities, those of sociopaths, of narcissists, and Machiavellians, are inherently manipulative. However, despite the harm that these types of personalities can do on others, we can also learn from them.

We can learn about how people work and what makes the minds of others tick. We can learn how people can be influenced, and from studying and learning from these people, we can also learn how to influence people for the better. Think about it— if you know that you can alter the opinion of someone else that is currently self-destructing, would you feel warranted in it? Is it warranted to influence, or even manipulate the feelings of someone else because you are sure that you will give them a better outcome?

With great power comes great responsibility, and as you learn to manipulate the minds of other people, you can also realize that you have the ability to influence and sway people—for better or for worse. You can convince someone else to do something that is naturally destructive or manipulative, or you can encourage them to do something that you know will make them happier, influencing them to act in ways that you know will help them.

Within this book, you will start to get a taste of exactly this; you will start to discover how dark psychology and manipulation exist. You will learn all about how manipulation is possible, how it works, and why it works the way it does, as well as the signs to note if someone else is attempting to manipulate you. This is essential information for you—you need to know what is going on so that you can guarantee that you can protect yourself. Manipulation itself is not inherently evil or problematic—it is the act of molding someone else to your liking. It is to shape them, much like how you can manipulate clay or other building materials. It does not have to be inherently dangerous or hurtful—though it certainly can be.

You will learn about why we are so vulnerable to dark psychology in this book, diving into understanding that ultimately, the way that people's minds work leaves them open. You will learn how to spot the red flags and note the effects of being manipulated as well. This will help you to discover several common tactics typically used by manipulators. You will also discover how to take control of those tactics yourself.

You will learn about the narcissists, naturally manipulative people that cannot help the way that they behave. You will be able to understand how to handle these narcissistic personalities to protect yourself, as well as how malignant narcissism can be so incredibly dangerous as you are hit with it.

We will take some time to look at neuro-linguistic programming, a type of subtle influencing technique that will allow you to alter the mind of someone else, encouraging them to do whatever it is that you want to by learning to communicate with their subconscious minds instead, entirely bypassing conscious detection, and we will then apply this to hypnosis as well.

From there, we will discuss the art of deception and how it can, arguably, fall into the dark types of behaviors that are commonly found within the dark triad of personalities. We will discover how deception is used, as well as explore the potential utilizations that exist. We will see how deception is able to be used readily and why people fall for it as well.

There will be some time spent upon the act of brainwashing and how it can be used so readily as well. We will look into the scientific evidence that goes into the process, followed by also understanding the challenges that come with it, comparing the differences between brainwashing and true mind control and how they differ.

We will take a look at how to read other people, taking into consideration the importance of body language, especially in the context of NLP and other forms of manipulation that are designed to influence the mind through the subconscious subtly, and that tends to happen through the use of body language. We communicate and respond primarily through the use of nonverbal communication—and we don't even realize it half of the time, creating the potent situation in which it is so easy to use to manipulate others.

Finally, as the book comes to a close, it will be time to consider how to regain control of your life so that you can protect yourself from manipulation before people have the chance to hurt you. We will also take a look at several tricks and tips that can go into keeping yourself safe from harm. We will be diving into tried and true tactics that can protect you from the devious attempts to influence and control you so that you know that you can be completely protected when it matters the most.

This book is different than the others—you will not only be learning to understand the tactics but why they work the way that they do. You will see what it is that makes the human mind, as powerful as it is, so susceptible to manipulation and being controlled by others.

You will also discover how you can use those very same tactics that go into controlling and sometimes even hurting other people for the betterment of your peers. You will learn how you can better influence the people around you. You will be taking the pages from the dark personality types and putting them to work for you so that you can know that you are in control.

There are plenty of books on this subject on the market, thanks again for choosing this one! Every effort was made to ensure it is full of as much useful information as possible; please enjoy it!

Chapter 1: Why Are We Vulnerable to Dark Psychology?

Now, let's begin—first, we are going to take a close look at dark psychology itself. Dark psychology is defined as the study of the dark personality types that exist in the dark triad of personality types. There are dark people in this world—predators, monsters in human clothing, who would like nothing more than to sink their teeth into their prey.

They target similar people, which is why once you have found yourself in a manipulative relationship, you will probably find that it happens again and again. This is not necessarily your fault—manipulators typically take what makes us the best versions of ourselves that we are and turn it into something that they can use to control you. They find ways to influence and control you that are different than the ones you could have ever imagined, and as a direct result, you find yourself caught off guard, unaware, and falling into their every trap.

We are, for the most part, quite susceptible to manipulation, despite the assertion that we are better than that. Even though you may assert to yourself that you are above petty control tactics that will keep you down, that is not the case at all. You must be willing to see how you can better interact with yourself and with those around you if you want to be able to control yourself. Within this chapter, we are going to explore those vulnerabilities, but first, we must take a look at the definition of manipulation itself. From there, we will address the most common red flags—the signs that you are currently being manipulated, as well as what manipulation and dark psychology can do to you.

Understanding Manipulation

Manipulation is, by definition, a form of social influence. Its entire purpose is to influence the behaviors, or the perceptions, of the people around the manipulator. Typically, the methods for manipulation are inherently deceptive, a topic that we will be addressing in depth when we get to Chapter 7. They can vary greatly from being somewhat innocuous to the point that most people tell you that you are overthinking things, or they can be overtly problematic as well, such as being blackmailed or threatened into submission. There are so many different forms of manipulation, and the vast majority of them are emotional.

If you have ever been on the receiving end of manipulation before, you probably know too well the struggles that you can face. It is difficult to understand what is happening. You probably doubt yourself. You tell yourself not to overreact, or you try to sweep everything under the rug to protect yourself. And yet, even if you know that you are being manipulated, you may still find yourself giving into the problems.

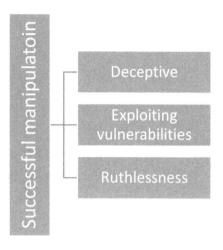

Manipulation works best when three criteria are met to allow for it to occur. The process is effective for these three simple reasons:

1. The manipulator must be willing to hide his or her true intentions—they are kept pushed away to deny the truth.

2. The manipulator must know what the vulnerabilities of the victim are so that they can then be exploited to get the results that the individual wants.

3. The manipulator must be ruthless enough to be willing to use those exploited vulnerabilities for his or her gains.

When this all works together, you will find that you are far more likely to give in to the manipulation. It makes sense, after all—when your manipulator hides their intention, typically, they are doing so because they know that if they tell you what they want, you will just refuse.

This is because we are typically contrarian in nature—we don't want to feel like we are giving someone else authority over ourselves, and that is exactly where reverse psychology gets its power. When your manipulator knows what your typical vulnerabilities are, they can be used against you to get you to simply give in to whatever demands the other party has without you being able to resist at all. We'll be addressing those vulnerabilities shortly. Finally, the manipulator has to not feel bad about what they are doing. When they feel bad about it, they will unintentionally betray themselves, and they will lose that power entirely. They need to maintain that ruthlessness; it makes it so that their guilt does not detract from the entire process. It is only when they can be ruthless about things that they can be as successful as they are.

This means that when someone can meet those three criteria, they have created the perfect breeding ground for disaster. They have just set themselves up to have that power over you. If you are completely unsuspecting and a particularly agreeable person, which most of the most common manipulation targets are, you will find that you give them exactly what they want. You allow them to manipulate you, albeit unknowingly, and as a direct result, they can take that control and run with it.

Vulnerabilities

Now, you, like most other people, probably think that you are a pretty steady person. You probably believe that you are not likely to be swayed or taken advantage of too easily. However, most people believe this—most people believe that they are likely to resist manipulation. They don't realize when they do have vulnerabilities, leaving them wide open to exploitation, and manipulators with malicious intent typically can sniff out the reason behind the actions with ease.

They can identify those vulnerabilities and take complete advantage of them so easily that you never even realize or suspect it, and that is where they get their power. Manipulators all tend to go for very similar people, and they typically have very predictable vulnerabilities. Let's look at some of the most common.

The need to please

Perhaps the easiest victims of manipulation are those that feel a constant need to please. They are constantly driven forward by this need to make people around them happy. Often, these people are quite naïve; they believe that it is the case that they are only good for making sure that those around them are pleased. Usually, they fear conflict and find that it is vastly easier to give in to conflict than it is to figure out how to avoid the problem entirely through giving in to whatever everyone around them wants.

The need for approval

Similarly, some people feel that they must earn the approval of others—they find that they only have any real value when other people believe that they are okay or that other people are accepting them. Their self-esteem is typically drawn entirely by making sure that other people are willing and able to please them, so they find that approval is the only way that they can feel good about themselves.

The fear of negative emotions

When it comes to negative emotions, some people become phobic of them—they are terrified of running into these negative associations with other people and want to do their best to figure out how to avoid triggering negative feelings from other people. They want to make sure that they can avoid being the target of disapproval, frustration, or anger, and so they will give in to whatever the manipulators request of them in hopes of being able to do better.

An inability to be assertive

Some people are simply what are known colloquially as doormats—they are too weak to say no to other people, usually for any number of reasons on this list. They may find that they need approval, they are afraid of negativity, or any other reason. No matter the reason for their lack of assertiveness, however, they are easy targets for manipulators and are typically favored for that reason.

Weak or no personal boundaries

Similarly, people who struggle with asserting and maintaining their boundaries tend to find that they struggle to protect themselves from manipulation.

Boundaries, as you will come to find over time, are perhaps the biggest threats to manipulators of all time. When someone has strong personal boundaries, they can keep themselves separate from the wills of other people. They can prevent themselves from falling victim to the ways that people tend to treat them because they will not allow things to get bad enough to let them be victimized in the first place. When those boundaries are missing, however, the manipulator has the perfect storm to simply steamroll over the victim to take control.

Low self-reliance

Self-reliance is something that everyone needs and yet is so hard to maintain. If you do not feel like you can rely on yourself, there is a good chance that you will find yourself taken advantage of. Feeling like you cannot trust yourself, that you are always wrong when you do something, is perhaps one of the best ways for you to end up the victim of a manipulator at some point.

A natural naïveté

When the target is naturally too naïve to understand what is happening around them or is likely to constantly give the other person the benefit of the doubt, they are going to end up victimized. The common belief behind this is that he or she would not do something nefarious, so why would anyone else? It is so easy to take advantage of people who always want to see the best in someone else.

Being overly conscientious

Similarly, some people always want to give those around them the benefit of the doubt. When something goes wrong, they assume that it was unintentional. They assume that when someone does something to them, they can justify it somehow, saying that the manipulator probably didn't mean it, or that it was probably an accident. They are so quick to try to see the side of the manipulator that they unintentionally throw themselves under the bus.

Lacking self-confidence

People lacking in self-confidence are too quick to let themselves talk themselves out of believing what is happening. They will readily tell themselves that they must have been at fault because they are *always* at fault. Their beliefs that they can never do anything right typically make them very easy for manipulators to take advantage of.

Submissive personality type

Some people have what is known as a submissive personality. They naturally give other people what they want, and they are quick to let themselves depend on other people to make all of the decisions and choose out everything that will happen. They are so dependent upon the other person that they often end up exploited and manipulated, even though they really should have been able to avoid the problem in the first place.

Red Flags of Manipulation

For those that *are* manipulated, it typically presents with several red flags that you might quickly sort of wave away, denying that they are a problem, but if you were honest with yourself, you would see that actually, there are many red flags all along the way. Some of them might be somewhat innocuous at first, but if you learn to identify them, you can start to protect yourself as well.

If you are worried that you may be the victim of manipulation for any reason, you should always attempt to address the reasons for the feelings so that you can take the necessary measures to defend yourself if necessary. After all, you owe it to yourself to make sure that you are protected. Even better, as you get better at spotting the signs that you are being manipulated in the first place, you can start to stop it before it happens. Let's take some time to identify those common red flags that you are likely to encounter along the way.

They make you feel insecure

No matter if the manipulator is a family member, a partner, a friend, or a coworker, you will notice that when you are around them, you will always feel insecure. They will leave you constantly feeling insecure no matter what you do, and that can be a huge problem. It is also a huge red flag, especially if before meeting that person, you were always completely comfortable with yourself.

They make you feel pressured

Manipulators love to make you feel pressured—they will lay it on regularly because they have little interest in actually pursuing anything meaningful with you. All they care about is getting you to cater to their whims, and if that means that they need to lay on the pressure, they are perfectly happy doing so.

They make you feel crazy

Manipulators tend to use a tactic called gaslighting. We will be going into this in more depth later, but essentially, it is a tactic in which the manipulator will tell you that things are not how you perceive them. His goal is to leave you feeling like you can't trust yourself or your perception of reality; he wants you to doubt that you are recalling what is happening so that he can take complete advantage of you.

They use statistics constantly to overwhelm you

You may find that the manipulator will constantly, in an argument, inundate you with statistics that may or may not be accurate or in context to try to force you to give in. They do this in all sorts of different ways in hopes of keeping control of you. After all, you can't argue with logic and numbers, can you? The manipulator will take advantage of the fact that most people won't stop to consider correlation vs. causation.

They are passive-aggressive

Typically, manipulators will lay on the passive-aggressive attitudes if they think that you won't give them what they want. They will hope that the pressure will make you cave; they rely on making you feel bad or undermined so that they will get what they need or want from you. They have no qualms with taking advantage of you, and this is one of the easiest ways that they can do so.

They make you feel judged or criticized

Manipulators will also lay on the judgment or criticism in hopes of making you feel more likely to give them what they want. They know that if they can make you feel like they are constantly judging you, you are far more likely to bow to their demands just because you will often be sensitive to that. No one likes feeling judged, after all, and that means that most manipulators have a very easy built-in weapon that they can take advantage of to control other people.

They insist that you speak first

If you find that the other person always wants you to speak first, just to criticize and tear apart everything that you say, they are probably trying to manipulate you. It is a method that works to make you feel dragged down or like you can't voice your complaints or disagreements. When this happens, you will find that you are constantly at the mercy of the other person and may even stop trying to justify yourself and what you have done out of fear of being torn down again and again. It becomes easier just not to share your thoughts or opinions at all.

They get loud or aggressive if you don't give them their way

Typically, you will find that manipulators will very quickly shift over to yelling or being aggressive if they are not getting their way. They will feel like they have no choice but to escalate further if that is what it will take to get you to obey. Typical manipulators will start with the least amount of force possible as they escalate up, trying to get you to do whatever it is that they want. There are typically no real qualms about having to get louder or more aggressive if that is what it will take. They will suddenly go from 0 to intimidatingly aggressive in the blink of an eye, leaving you confused, hurting, and wondering what happened.

They pressure you to act quickly

You may find that your manipulator will also constantly weigh on you to make decisions quickly. The pressure is there to serve one simple purpose: Decisions made in times of heightened emotion are typically not as good as those that you can make when you have the time to mull over a decision. You might find that you get time limits to manipulate you or to get you to obey quicker than you intend to. They will set arbitrary limits in hopes of making you feel like you have to rush and, therefore, do not think over things in a very responsible manner. As a direct result, then they get to have some degree of influence over the decision that you make.

They insist on meeting in person to argue

Finally, you will probably notice that all of the arguments or confrontations that you have are in person—and on the other person's terms. The manipulator wants that home-field advantage— they want to take you somewhere that you are not completely comfortable in so that they can take advantage of what is going on. They want to be able to essentially belittle you into their decision or to get you to give in to them, so they make it a point to bring you somewhere that they are comfortable and you are not. Further, they usually are masters at using body language to intimidate and dominate over their victims, and that requires them to be in your general presence to be effective.

Chapter 2: Commonly Used Manipulative Tactics

When it comes to being the victim of manipulation, your attackers have no shortage of options available to them. They can manipulate you in a myriad of ways to make you feel like you are stuck, down, or unable to do whatever it is that you intended or wanted. Your manipulator is a master at making you feel controlled. He or she is a skilled, natural influencer, able to identify weakness and take advantage without ever feeling a single bit of remorse.

Would a wolf feel bad as it took down a sheep for its dinner? Not at all—and similarly speaking, dark personality types of all kinds will not care about taking advantage of you either. They see you as little more than a means to an end. Even if they make you feel like you are loved at first, they have no intention of maintaining a relationship long-term. They want you around just long enough to get what they want, and when you no longer of use to them, you will almost always be discarded and thrown away. They will not bother to keep you around at all, a testament to just how little they care about their victims.

For manipulators, everything is tactical— everything has a very specific purpose that they are trying to meet. They will intentionally do whatever it will take to meet their demands, no matter the impact that it will have on other people, and they have no problems hurting others if that is what it will take.

This particular chapter will explore some of the more common tactics that manipulators typically use to browbeat targets into submission in an attempt to get them to feel like they have no choice but to give in to get through the situation. This is by no means a comprehensive list—there are hundreds of different kinds of manipulative tactics that exist to influence and control people. However, these are some of the ones that you are the most likely to encounter during your life.

Isolation

We are a very social species—we always want to work to foster relationships with other people. This is the natural order of humans in general; we just want to make sure that we can interact with each other, and that requires us to make concessions sometimes. We know this, and we usually will have no problems sometimes compromising to keep those groups. However, social groups also represent protection and power. When you are in a group of people that all care about you, they will be on the lookout for anything that might harm you. They will do what they can to protect you because they want to keep you safe.

Manipulators hate victims that have plenty of close relationships with other people because it is so much harder to manipulate people when there are others around them, calling people out and telling them not to do something. When you are in a group with other people, you will find that it is easy for others to come to your defense, and it is easy to feel empowered to defend yourself. They will be there, backing you up and reminding you that you are on the right track or that you should stick to your guns if you are insisting on one thing that contradicts your manipulator. Because of the backup that you will have in close groups, it becomes easier to simply segregate a victim off and break away those close relationships instead of disrupting them.

When a manipulator isolates their victims from others, they are making it a point to cut off those important connections. They may stir up trouble or insist that their victims end all of their relationships that they have. They may tell you that it is them or your friends or family. They may insist that you will end a relationship because they tell you that you are untrustworthy, and they will not stop until you give in. They want you to have as little emotional support as possible. If you only have them to fall back on, your natural inclination to stay close to people kicks in, and you are much more likely to back down and listen.

Additionally, when your relationships are limited, the manipulator can limit the flow of information and the narrative that they will use to control their victim. As we will address within this chapter, repetition becomes a valuable asset. If all you ever hear is what your manipulator says, then there is a big problem—you will find yourself naturally agreeing or even following along with what is being said. This is all because you are only ever exposed to that belief set, so naturally, you absorb it.

This is why, so often, manipulators will work hard to cut off access to family. They will weave narratives about how your best friend hates them, or that your family only wants you to break up with them. They will push it into an "us vs. the world" narrative in which everything is worded as you and your manipulator going up against everyone else to isolate you.

Criticism

You will commonly see manipulators wielding criticisms to control people as well. No one likes to feel criticized—it makes them feel like they have been treated poorly or like they are unappreciated. Think about the last time that you felt criticized— it probably felt awful. You probably did something that you hoped would be appreciated, only to find that really, the other person was annoyed or told you that you weren't good enough.

With criticism, you find that you are stuck feeling like you are never good enough. You might do one thing that your manipulator wants from you, only to realize that he has suddenly changed the goalposts and now wants even more from you. Think of it this way—imagine that your partner has requested that you make sure that you cook dinner and have it done at 6:00 exactly every single day. You are busy, but you find a way to make it happen, knowing that it matters to your partner, and so you do it. You make sure that dinner is made at exactly 6 in the evening the next day when he walks in the door... And he is still not satisfied.

You expected him to praise you, to be happy, and to thank you for the effort. After all, you had to change around what you were doing just to make that work for you. Your partner takes a bite and crinkles his nose, telling you that you over-salted the meat and that it is really bland, salty, burnt, but somehow raw in the center at the same time, leaving you feeling bad, frustrated, and probably even inadequate.

You did what he asked, and while you might not be the best cook, certainly it wasn't that bad, was it? However, he insists that he is right and that you should feel terrible about what you made. He leaves you feeling like cooking something simple isn't good enough-you had to do more than that, and you dropped the ball, and because of that, he is frustrated. He tells you that you need to make sure that the food is perfect, delicious, and worth the money that he would spend on it.

You feel criticized and bad. This only serves to make you feel less confident about yourself. You let him break down your self-esteem and therefore are more likely to try to please him in hopes of being able to avoid being the victim of the next argument as well.

Alternatively, criticism can work toward other people, too—it can be used to point out examples of other people to make you feel like you are segregated. "Oh, well, you know, it could be worse. I could be like *John*. You know, constantly yelling and throwing things. You're lucky that I'm so good to you and that I make sure that your home is as comfortable as I do. You know, other men wouldn't be so good to you." This is done to make you further align with your manipulator or to make you feel like you are lucky to be in the position that you are. It is once again that us vs. them mentality that was mentioned earlier.

Peer Pressure

Peer pressure is incredibly powerful—we all have this inherent need to be liked, and peer pressure allows for that to be exploited and controlled. When it comes to peer pressure, you will find that people are far more likely to agree to something that they don't want to do when they realize that their peers are doing them as well. This is actually a common form of persuasion in general—you make it clear to someone that other people in their demographics are doing something, and they begin to feel like that is what is expected of them, making them more likely to give in, whether they want to or not.

Think of how, in high school, you can end up with a group of kids all doing something that no one wants to do, all because they think that it is expected or because they think that the only way that they will be liked or accepted is if they give in and do what everyone else is doing. In reality, they are all miserable, only doing what they do in hopes of being a part of the 'in' crowd.

You can see this same effect commonly with manipulators. They may want you to do something, and when you protest, they point out why you are wrong. They point out how everyone else is doing it, so why shouldn't you? "You know, even John's girlfriend is willing to do that. Why aren't you? I've never met someone unwilling before. Can't you just give it a shot? Everyone else does it, so it can't be that bad." This kind of narrative is incredibly harmful, especially when the victim is already isolated and feeling criticized. They are much more likely to give in because they feel like they have no other choice in the situation.

They feel trapped, like if they don't give in, they are only going to make the situation worse, or that they will be the odd one out that was the buzzkill or the party pooper.

Fear of Alienation

Similarly, to peer pressure, fear of alienation can also be manipulated easily. Typically, when you first meet the manipulator, you will find that you have met a person that appears to be kind, fun, and someone that you like or want to hang around. You start to think that he or she is probably great—after all, look at everything that he is doing? A common tactic is to make use of what is known as love-bombing—the tactic in which an individual tries to win your affections and loyalty through making you feel loved and special in hopes of manipulating those feelings later on. Your manipulator might have taken you out to special dinners or showered you with lavish gifts.

Over time, you start to feel attached and like you want to stay with this person, but then they start to change up what they are doing. They start to manipulate you, and when you try to push back, or you ask them not to make you do something, they tell you that they will leave. They threaten to walk out of a relationship or to shut you out entirely. Especially if you have already been isolated, you will find that the fear of being entirely alienated is too much—you comply because you don't want to be alone.

This commonly relies on tactics such as the silent treatment or devaluing someone else. The whole point is to make the individual feel the pressure of being abandoned or all alone in hopes of taking advantage more in the future. The manipulator is hoping to find a way to take complete control over the situation, and what better way than to make you feel like you are going to be dropped if you don't give in quickly? Even if you don't really want to, the alternative of living without that person seems unpleasant enough to pressure you into doing whatever you were told.

Repetition

Repetition is highly powerful, especially as persuasion. It works quite simply—when you make it a point to repeat something to someone enough times, they will naturally start to believe it, especially if you are slow and subtle about how you bring it up and how you use the information that you are providing. In particular, you are likely to see that people will make it a point to use repetition to push new ideas into someone else's mind. Now, you might think that this is silly—can't you just resist and tell yourself that something is false?

While you can resist, to some extent, your unconscious mind is always paying attention to what is happening around you. It is constantly learning and absorbing information. It does not differentiate between good and bad or right or wrong; the more that something or some type of subject is repeated to your mind, the more likely you are to believe it. This is exactly how mantras and affirmations work—they are designed to convince you through sheer repetition that you should believe something so that you can be able to change your mind from the inside out.

While this can be great for you if you are setting good affirmations for yourself, it is also dangerous if you find that people around you constantly expose you to less well-intentioned ideas. When you constantly hear the same negative emotions or messages thrown toward you over and over again, you will start to believe them.

If you catch that you are constantly having the same talks and the same messages pushed toward you, there is a great chance that in reality, you are just being manipulated. This has nothing to do with you, and you can't really fight it off, even if you are constantly consciously aware of it. You will eventually start to pick up on the messages, even if only subconsciously, and that can be a huge problem. This is why it is always so much better to avoid manipulators.

Fatigue

When you are tired, you are naturally more suggestible. This is because your brain just isn't working as efficiently as it should be. When you are tired, it is difficult to continue to police yourself over time; you are more likely to just give in to what is being said to you so that you can move on. Your brain simply wants to get to sleep.

It has been shown in studies that at the point of being awake for just 21 hours, you are already more susceptible to persuasive measures, such as repetition. This is commonly utilized during brainwashing, and perhaps the most popular that is known is through the use of manipulating cults. When forming cults, especially those malignant ones that push harmful ideas, the cult leaders work to indoctrinate their followers, often through forms of physical impairment, such as being sleep deprived. The more sleep deprived that you are, the more likely that you are to absorb and accept the message.

You can get a similar effect with other forms of need deprivation. Most notably, when intoxicating someone else, with alcohol or other mind-altering drugs, you can get very similar states of suggestibility. People will naturally become more agreeable naturally, shifting toward those tendencies because they are not thinking rationally and with their whole brains. Be mindful of those that work to keep you awake, even when you desperately need sleep. They are dangerous individuals that can very heavily influence you and your behaviors. They know what they are doing, and you need to be able to get sleep whenever you can.

Forming New Identities

Another common form of manipulation is the act of forming new identities, typically through processes such as mind control. The idea here is that manipulators want to find a way to re-define you. They want to sculpt you, to manipulate you into exactly what they want, and they want to make sure that you are as obedient and useful as possible. Now, it is socially unacceptable to physically beat you into submission or to torture someone into fearing the manipulator enough to listen to everything that is ordered. Because of that, typically, they go for tactics that are not as likely to be prosecuted as a crime. Though just as nefarious, mental warfare and emotional abuse don't leave physical, visible signs that something has happened, meaning that they can be used effectively without there ever being any evidence of abuse occurring in the first place.

Through the use of mind control, manipulators can start to encourage and manipulate you into doing what they want, when they want it. They effectively work to destroy your personality and your current self as much as they can so that they can then build you from the bottom up. They work through all sorts of different tactics and techniques to effectively get you to disown the past you, to denounce the person that you were. When you start to doubt yourself, you can then be used and influenced to becoming what the manipulator wants.

Now, it is important to note that this does differ from brainwashing, a tactic that is used and preys upon self-preservation instincts. Instead of trying to mentally break you into thinking that you have no possible out and that you must assimilate or die, mind control seeks to happen more covertly and with fewer threats. Typically, mind control involves first making sure that the manipulator is deemed a person of trust—by being trustworthy, he or she can ensure that you do not suspect them as a potential manipulator in the first place.

Typically, forming new identities is quite involved—it requires a long-term commitment and is typically only really reserved for people being groomed into being a longer-term partner or spouse to the manipulator. They will do this to make sure that they can get whatever it is that they want out of the relationship without worrying too much about the repercussions. They will usually work to install buttons, so to speak, to get you to do what they want when they want it. Through doing so, they are able to effectively mold a person into being exactly what it is that they want in a partner, meaning that they have a constant supply of whatever it is that they want. They find ways to force people to bend to their wills, and in doing so, they end up successfully holding all of the keys that they needed.

During this process, then, the individual manipulator will go through the following steps to take control of the other person. Keep in mind that this is a relatively simplistic outline of the process—but it does more or less cover the basics of what you can expect to happen.

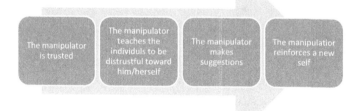

The manipulator is trusted — The manipulator teaches the individuls to be distrustful toward him/herself — The manipulator makes suggestions — The manipulatior reinforces a new self

1. **The manipulator becomes trusted:** The manipulator cannot get their way unless they are someone that the victim trusts. This is because they need to be at a point of being able to directly talk to and

influence the other person's mind as they want to in order to organically change the mindset of their victim.

2. **The manipulator establishes distrust in oneself:** The manipulator will then work to sort of discredit their victim's personality. They may start to break down self-esteem, for example, or criticize the other person enough to make them star to doubt what they are doing. The more that they start to hate themselves, the easier it is to detach and reject the old self to absorb the new one. The whole point is to make the victim believe that they are the problem here— their own mindsets are working against them and that their own natural mindsets are the reasons for their failures.

3. **The manipulator makes suggestions:** Carefully, then, when the victim is highly distrustful of themselves or doubting themselves enough to start to self-hate, the manipulator is then able to

start making all sorts of suggestions to the victim to get them to start taking on new beliefs, likes, and more. This is usually done through criticizing other people, through pointing out things that the manipulator does like, making suggestions directly, and even encouraging the individual that is being manipulated to also make it a point to change up what they are doing. They offer all sorts of solutions, and as a trusted individual thanks to step 1 of this process, most of the time, the manipulator can succeed accordingly. There is also usually some repetition happening as well in hopes of really driving those points home effectively.

4. **The manipulator reinforces the new self:** Then, with the victim starting to live up to what the manipulator wanted, they now have to praise and further encourage the victim to really reinforce the changes. The more praise that the victim gets from the manipulator, especially with that

position of power, the more reinforced those changes become, and the more likely that they are to continue the changes long-term.

As you can see, this can be highly effective in changing someone completely. This is exactly how, all too often, you see people saying that they don't know what happened or how they changed over time—they became someone entirely different from the individual that they once knew, and they never suspect a thing. If they do start to worry about abuse or manipulation, they don't ever assume that it is coming from the manipulators themselves because they are in positions of trust, making this even more insidious than before.

Deception

Finally, when you look at common manipulation tactics, you will see the deception. This particular one is highly powerful. It works well to make people think one-way or believe words that are not truthful. Especially when told by someone trustworthy, deception is highly effective—so effective that we will be dedicating an entire chapter to this subject. Chapter 7 is all about various deceptive strategies that are commonly used.

Chapter 3: Common Signs of Being Manipulated

Manipulation can have some very real, very insidious implications for those that find themselves on the receiving ends. It is hurtful. It is destructive. It can even cause lifelong effects that can be entirely devastating to the individuals suffering. When you are manipulated, you are not only controlled and influenced; you are also directly betrayed. Most forms of manipulation require some sort of trust to be effective in the first place, and because of that, the trust is violated. Manipulation can be entirely detrimental to those that are finding themselves on the receiving end of the abuse, and they may not even realize that they were hit with it in the first place.

Usually, the victims rarely actually notice the signs in themselves—it is other people on the peripheral of the relationship that start to notice or question it. Friends might ask you why you have been down so much. Family members might point out that you are changing. Your coworkers may ask you if everything is okay, but you are oblivious, not fully aware of the changes that are happening until it is too late. You don't realize just how much harm you are enduring when you live with or are close to a manipulator.

We are taught to love others around us unconditionally; we learn that we should always believe that people who love us don't want to hurt us, and because of that, we end up more vulnerable. We end up disregarding the abuse and the manipulation until it is far too late, and there can be permanent impacts from it. It can damage your capacity to love and trust, and it can even leave you feeling inherently broken or worthless as well. It is so important for you to be able to look at yourself in the mirror, and manipulation can ruin that for the victims.

The truth is, while most typically functioning individuals will not go out of their ways to use and abuse, the manipulators will. There is always the potential that you are working with a manipulator, and that potential is something that you have to be aware of.

This is why it becomes so important for anyone to know what the most common signs of abuse and manipulation are, especially because it doesn't leave bruises. There aren't physical marks there to show the world that you are being hurt by someone else. However, there are very distinctive mental marks that, if you can identify them, you will be able to use to your advantage. You can learn to recognize what is happening—you can learn to see those signs so that if they start to arise in you or in someone that you love, you can point them out and get that help sooner rather than later. By being aware of the potential for abuse and the warning signs, you can be certain that you protect yourself and your loved ones.

Before we begin this chapter, please know that if you were on the receiving end of manipulation or abuse, you were not asking for it. Note that you are not the one at fault here, nor is trusting someone that you thought you could trust or that cared about you a crime that you should be punished for. Remember that often, the manipulators in our lives are those that are highly likely to cause all sorts of problems for us, but that is not our fault, nor do we have to feel bad or ashamed about it when it does happen. Now, let's start to get to work on identifying those signs.

If you are being made to feel like you have to question yourself, like you have no choice but to give in to what the other person is saying, there is a very good chance that you are being manipulated or otherwise controlled. Dark psychology can be great sometimes—it can really help to understand behavior and how to influence people to do the right thing. However, sometimes, you have to realize that it can be harmful as well. It is very easy for manipulation, in particular, to weigh heavily on the person that is being controlled. Because of that, you must learn to avoid it. Let's take a look at some of the ways that dark psychology can be used to cause harm to the victims.

Feeling Confused

Manipulation is confusing for just about anyone. It is hard to go from thinking that someone in your life loved and supported you but is now hurting you without any sort of confusion. Frequently, you feel like your world has been turned upside down, especially with those different tendencies and tactics that were likely thrown your way. If you were ever the victim of gaslighting, you probably doubt yourself. You probably feel like you are to blame or that you made your partner like this. You probably feel like you are hurting or like you don't know up from down anymore. Rest assured, this is typical in these situations, and you are not alone. However, you should make it a point to change. Don't let yourself fall for these habits long-term. Let this be the red flag that you need to see that the manipulation is there.

When you are in the throes of manipulation and abuse, it is very easy not to know what to expect or how to behave. It becomes very easy for you to feel like ultimately, you are stuck on a rollercoaster, and you can't understand how things got to where they are. At this point, you probably liked, trusted, or even loved, the manipulator, and you find yourself wondering why someone that you loved or trusted suddenly has become this monster that seems determined to break you down and destroy you.

Questioning Yourself

Similarly, you probably find yourself wondering if everything that you experienced in your time with the manipulator was what you thought it was. Did you do something that set them off? Did you ask for it? Could you have changed things if you were a bit stronger? "If only I did x instead of y..." you might lament to yourself, but really, that is not fair to you. It is not your fault, and you did not make your manipulator choose to influence or control you.

You may feel like you can't trust yourself when you are trying to recall an event. This is especially true if you are constantly gaslit into believing whatever it is that the manipulator insists is the case. You find that it is easier to question yourself, to blame yourself for what is happening than to accept that the fault lies with the manipulator. You then ask if you had everything to do with everything that ever happened to you—you point out how ultimately, you must have been at fault just by virtue of what happened and because your manipulator has said that much.

Feeling Anxious or Hypervigilant

Being manipulated is traumatic, especially when it comes from someone that you loved or trusted. It is so easy for you to feel like you are unable to trust others after this; you will probably feel like you were wrong once before, so you have to be on guard for this so that it doesn't happen again in the future. This is not really something that anyone can fault you for; of course, you are worried about being victimized again. However, if you are not careful, you can have some worse effects.

You may start to suffer from anxiety—and who can blame you? If you are constantly being betrayed and manipulated by someone that you assumed you could trust, of course, you will feel like you need to guard yourself against other forms of manipulation that could come your way. You try to protect yourself by overcorrecting—instead of being too trusting, you become hypervigilant. Unfortunately, the result is anxiety that can be entirely devastating if you don't take care of it accordingly.

Keep in mind that even just constantly being manipulated can cause you to be anxious as well; you can feel like you are constantly having to be cautious about what is going on. You can find that you feel like you have one choice but to be worrying about what is going on, and you can constantly be watching for signs that your partner is going to snap at you again.

Feeling Ashamed or Guilty

No one wants to admit that they were made a victim. It is almost discouraged in this day and age, especially because most people how have never been there before are so quick to ask you why you would possibly put yourself in that position in the first place. They are all so quick to ask why you would seek out someone like an abuser or a manipulator, despite not realizing that most of them wear highly attractive masks. They don't get that ultimately; the manipulator doesn't get other people to stick around them through being abusive or manipulative the first time he or she meets the other person. It takes time to build up to that level. They are great at playing the long game. Especially in relationship settings, you will find that manipulators will work hard to be perfect at first. They want to build that emotional attachment before they start to turn on their victim, and often, the victim is left entirely blindsided to what just happened—they didn't realize that would happen, nor did they have any way of knowing.

You may find that you constantly feel dirty, ashamed, or guilty about what has happened. You must have been at fault, you tell yourself—you must have been the cause to it all, and because of that, you feel guilty or even ashamed of yourself. You find that it is easier to blame yourself for causing the damage, or even for allowing yourself to be abused or used in the first place. As a direct result, you make yourself feel worse than you needed to, causing yourself even more problems than you needed. This can just exacerbate the entire situation.

Keep in mind that it is not your fault. You do not deserve to pay for your manipulator's crimes; if you have been influenced negatively or hurtfully in the past, you are not responsible for the actions of the other person. You can learn to do better as well; you can discover what it will take for you to move on, to become someone better, more stable, and more able to see the situation for what it is. You can better yourself so that you can avoid these problems in the future.

Becoming Passive or Submissive

When you are constantly being manipulated, especially with passive-aggressive or otherwise hurtful methods, you will probably find that you become passive. The longer that you are in with a manipulator or an abuser, the easier it becomes to simply give in. It is so much easier to just give in, to let your partner or manipulator have their way than it is to try to fight it or defend yourself. You find that it is so much easier than you don't even bother trying anymore.

Alternatively, you may learn that your needs are associated with pain or discomfort. You learn that your partner or manipulator will not be particularly sympathetic to you when you need something, and in fact, may berate or belittle you for having those needs in the first place. This is especially true with narcissists—who only want you around for them. It becomes so bad to try to get your way or get what you need that you eventually just stop trying. You become afraid or ashamed of the needs that you have, and you sit back quietly, waiting for your manipulator to tell you what to do next.

Taking action effectively becomes associated with pain, and because of that, passivity becomes the default coping mechanism. It is hard to act if you worry about what will happen next if you do, and you decide that at least you know what the current pain or discomfort is—that is better than the unknown that you will be exposed to if you try to vocalize your needs at all.

Feeling Like You Are on Eggshells

Similarly, you may find that you constantly feel like you are on eggshells. Your partner may constantly snap without any sort of warning. You may discover that your partner is not stable or reliable, and it is so much easier to just try to walk around them and their problems than it is to try to do what you want. It is easier to keep the peace by trying not to set off the other person.

However, this is problematic; you are always working in anticipation of being hurt. This usually carries over outside of that one context as well, and you very quickly find that you are constantly worrying about how you will be perceived and what you can do to avoid running into further problems. You will, in other contexts, attempt to avoid setting other people off as well, becoming a people pleaser. However, unfortunately, this just sets you up for more abuse and manipulation in the future. Remember, this people-pleasing attitude was one of those that was a big red flag that many manipulators look for to control their targets.

Feeling Numb

The longer that you spend in a relationship or around someone that never seems to care for your feelings and what you need, the more likely that you are to just give up on feeling in the first place. After all, emotions become dangerous weapons against you; with those emotions that you have, you are only feeling worse over time. You feel hopeless as the manipulation continues; you may not even really react much to the criticism anymore when it happens more and more.

This is known as dissociation; it is a common response to trauma of all kinds in which your body effectively chooses to shut down emotions rather than trying to process those painfully dangerous ones that could become problematic in all sorts of contexts throughout your life. You might start to feel numb in other relationships as well. You might stop trying to do anything that you once enjoyed. You may start becoming simply unresponsive in general. Nothing makes you feel happy anymore, so why even bother in the first place?

You eventually settle into this state of quiet apathy—at least in apathy, you have less pain.

Seeking Approval

When you are constantly being torn down in your relationships, you often get to a point in which you are constantly seeking approval from others. You effectively make all of your value being able to get that approval from other people, and the less that you get from others, the worse that you end up feeling.

Effectively, because you are so used to being belittled, made the problem, and even potentially blamed for what is happening to you and the interactions that you have, you start trying to do everything you can to just please everyone in your area. This is your coping mechanism to the manipulation and rejection—if you are constantly exceeding expectations, can anyone criticize you? If you are constantly doing what you must, can anyone get back at you or hurt you or fault you for it?

Once again, however, this is yet another potential risk factor for being manipulated again in the future. When you are constantly working to please everyone around you, what can you expect to get? You will constantly have people trying to use you and take advantage of you. The more that you do to please people and the less that you say no or try to set up boundaries, the more likely that you are to be victimized more in the future.

Remember, manipulators work through grooming their targets. If you weren't already a people-pleaser before being manipulated, you probably would be by the time that the manipulation is done just to protect yourself, especially from the constant criticism and isolation that you are probably subjected to. When the only way to get back to people and having that relationship is through people-pleasing, you will probably tend to do so. You want yourself to be as perfect as possible so that you will be appreciated—even if only briefly.

Resentment

As you are hit with all sorts of manipulation and abuse more and more often, you become more likely to become resentful of it as it occurs. This is because you don't want to be manipulated—and who can blame you? Resentment is pretty typical when you feel like you are in a bad situation. It may come through in different ways, and it may be aimed differently, but really, the resentment is just your frustration at the situation being funneled toward someone or something.

Resentment is how all of your negative emotions surrounding the entire situation are bottled up so that they can be purged. However, it is difficult to do this constructively. Resentment, while it serves its purpose of making you want to leave your current situation so that you can be in a better one, is also quite unhealthy to harbor, especially if it is toward yourself. You may start to resent yourself for not seeing the signs sooner or not being strong enough to leave the situation. You might resent your manipulator for being the way that he or she is. You might resent friends and family for not warning you of the red flags. It is important that, if you are resentful, you learn to process this the right way.

Most often, this comes out as frustration or irritation—you snap at yourself or those around you. You grow impatient with yourself and anything that you do, blaming yourself for what has happened. You are irritable and moody. You may even start to project those feelings toward people that had nothing to do with the situation at all.

Developing Depression or Anxiety

Some people become depressed or anxious after they have been manipulated or abused. It is easy to believe the lies that you were told to keep you down when they were repeated so much. It becomes easy to tell yourself that really, you are worthless for letting the situation get so bad or that it is your fault, and you deserved what happened to you. The more depressed that you get, however, the less likely that you are to seek help or try to escape.

You may feel like you are worthless or that you are too stressed out or anxious to do anything. You might withdraw and give up entirely, not seeing the value in trying any longer when nothing will ever change from your perspective. It becomes easier to just remain in the situation and resign to your fate, even though there is help out there and that no one deserves to live in constant stress.

Anxiety can be debilitating. It can lie to you and tell you that there is no escape. It can make you feel like things will only get worse if you try to do anything to defend yourself or to leave or make your situation better. Remember, anxiety is only there to lie to you. It isn't your friend. It isn't there to help you, and it is there to keep you back.

Self-sabotaging

When you are suffering in a manipulative situation, you may decide that there is no point in trying anymore. You may find that you simply give up because there is no point anyway. You acknowledge that your manipulator will never change, and because of that, you stop trying. However, is this the right option for you? Think about it—instead of making it a point to walk away from the situation; you have chosen to make yourself stuck in it longer.

When it comes right down to it, you have two options—you can stay, or you can go. However, no one can make you stay in a manipulative or abusive situation without your consent, whether you believe it or not. This is how manipulators get people in the first place—they make them want to stay. They make them feel like they need to stick around or that things will be better if they do, whether through threats or through constantly oscillating between manipulating and hurting the victim and showering them with love.

Remember, nothing in manipulation is unintentional; your manipulator is doing everything, knowing exactly what is being done. They are doing it on purpose to get their way. They have probably done it to other people before, and they will probably repeat it in the future. However, that does not have to be with you. You can break the cycle and change what you are willing to tolerate.

You can learn to do better for yourself simply by taking action in the first place. You can learn to pull away from the negativity. You can free yourself from the trap of manipulation, and this book will help you with that as you continue to read. You are not stuck. Nothing in life is permanent—even your abuse. While your manipulator may want you to feel that way, rest assured that you can learn to overcome it.

That is one of the primary purposes of this book—
we will be delving into what you can do to protect
yourself in the future. We will be looking at how,
with recognizing these signs, you can also start to
make the changes in your life that you want to see.
You can learn to fight the abuse and recognize it as
it happens. You can even learn the weapons of the
manipulator and dark abusers so that you can use
them yourself—for good.

It can be cathartic to take control of those same
tactics that controlled you for so long so that you
can turn them into something more. You can turn
them into something that can help other people.
You can use them to influence people to do the
right thing. You can also use some of the tools that
you will see in this book to help yourself as well.
Especially when we get to hypnosis and NLP, you
will be introduced to some tools that are highly
powerful and can be some of your greatest assets
when it comes to being able to change your life
forever. If you want to be able to beat the
manipulator, you need to beat them at their own
game—but that also means being willing to see the
difference between using tools such as influence

and manipulation for good and for nefarious purposes.

Chapter 4: Narcissism

Imagine that you have just met someone new. He is perfect he likes all of the same things that you do. He appreciates your jokes. He showers you with all sorts of lavish affection and attention, and because of that, you find yourself becoming more and more attached. However, what would you think if you realized that, behind that mask, behind that perfect face that you see there, was not the person that you thought, but a monster, waiting for the time to be right to strike?

The truth is, people with narcissism, or more formally, narcissistic personality disorder, are dangerous. Especially those with malignant narcissism tend to be entirely invested in just causing problems for the sake of problem causing in the first place. They must be the center of attention, in control of everything, and working to ensure that they are getting everything that they want.

Within this chapter, we are going to take a look at narcissists—they tend to be some of the most abusive, problematic people that you can face, and the worst part is, you rarely know that you have met one until it is too late. You are already too attached to just break off cleanly. This is by design, of course—the calculating narcissist knew exactly what was being done when this happened. The narcissist intentionally worked to do this, to get you invested so that he could then do whatever he wanted. It is how narcissists everywhere are able to keep people under their thumbs for so long in the first place. We will look at what narcissism is, what the most identifying traits are, and how they tent to abuse. We will consider the carryover into malignant narcissism as well, and finally, end on how to handle the narcissist to protect yourself from their abuse. When you know the warning signs and how to handle them, you can disarm the narcissist entirely, protecting yourself before you have to put up with any more abuse. The truth is, the narcissist is dangerous, and there is no reason that you should allow him to take advantage of you.

Defining Narcissism

Narcissistic personality disorder is quite simple—it is a condition in which people have a sense that they are more important than they are. Typically, they operate on the assumption that ultimately, they can do what they want, when they want it because they know that they are better than the rest. This is just one of three of the dark triad personality types that typically are seen with dark psychology, and the worst part is, the narcissist often doesn't even realize the full extent of what he is doing. He rarely thinks that the abuse that he is suffering is from a disorder in the first place. He assumes that his thoughts, feelings, and behaviors are exactly right, and those are assumed without empathy for what it could mean for others.

The narcissist is, in a word, self-absorbed. He cannot empathize for all sorts of different reasons that may be prevailing, but the truth is, he is unable to understand how other people feel—and he doesn't care to, either. He doesn't want to figure out what it will take for him to talk about what other people want or need because, to him, he is the most important one that is there.

To be clinically diagnosed with narcissism, one must be noted to have several defining traits that are looked at to consider narcissist tendencies. The diagnostic criteria include:

- **Grandiose sense of self-importance:** The narcissist believes, usually delusionally so, that he is the most important person in the world. He may very well be, too, but only to himself. He believes that he is the most critical person in any setting, no matter what the truth is. He will go out of his way to spin any tales that he needs to figure out how to pass himself off as the most important person, and he will do so in his ways, no matter the cost. He will believe, in a relationship, that he is the one pushing forward, that he is the more important one and that he is the only reason that the relationship works in the first place.

- **Obsession with unrealistic ideals:** Success, influence, power, love, a piece of arm candy... The narcissist believes that he deserves it all, and he will do whatever it takes to make sure that he makes it happen. He will obsess and idealize these unrealistic ideals in hopes of making them happen, but in reality, he can't have it all. No one can, and of course, that just serves as fuel for his idea that the world is unfair and harsh, and he isn't getting what he was owed.

- **Needs excessive admiration and attention:** The narcissist needs to feel valued to almost an extreme extent. He wants to get that admiration at all costs, and if you aren't constantly praising him, he will never be completely satisfied. He feeds off of reinforcement, positive and negative, and he will get it any way that he can.

- **Entitlement:** The narcissist believes that, inherently, as the best person out there and the only factor that makes anything work in the world, that he deserves everything that he wants. Pair this back to the second point, and you start to see the problem—he believes that he can have anything that he wants, and as a result, you run into a problem of not ever being able to satisfy the narcissist. He always believes that he wants more and that he deserves more, and he will obsess over it.

- **Manipulative by nature:** The narcissist, believing that he is deserving of everything, will also manipulate to get it. Most of the time, narcissists always have a reason for doing what they are doing. They will intentionally work toward manipulating when it is necessary and when it fits their agenda. However, they are also opportunistic; if you are of no use to the narcissist, you are more likely to be ignored than manipulated.

- **Lacking empathy:** Narcissists don't empathize. They might be able to understand what the other person is feeling, recognizing that ultimately, the annoyance or pain or anything else is being felt, but they also just don't care. It doesn't bother them to inflict pain. They don't feel bad when they see someone else crying. This is what makes them so dangerous, especially with the manipulation proclivity that they tend to show.

- **Envy-oriented:** The narcissist will usually be in one of two camps—they will believe that you either envy them for some reason, or they will be envious of what you have—at which point, they will somehow spin it around so, in reality, you are envious of them instead. They don't want to admit that someone else has it better than them, and they will do anything in their power to avoid doing so, even if that means delusionally convincing themselves that really, the problem is with the other person.

- **Haughty and arrogant:** The narcissist typically comes off as arrogant—because he believes that he is better than everyone else around him. He is aggressive toward people that don't just give in to what he wants. Look at his interactions toward people deemed as subservient, such as waiters or people in customer service—the narcissist will be awful to them more often than not, claiming that he is putting them in their place and that they deserve it.

Ultimately, the narcissist is not a very kind person to be around, but the truth is, he usually can't help it. Of course, that just makes him all the more dangerous—he acts in these manners unintentionally, without malice. He is simply destructive, and he is dangerous to be in a relationship with. His entire worldview, that paradigm that he uses to see the world, is just inherently skewed, and there is nothing that you can do about that to fix it. The best that you can do is hope to steer clear, or to learn several tools that you can use to try to mitigate the damage that he would otherwise do.

Narcissistic Traits

Typically, there are several defining traits that may not be particularly important to diagnosis but are highly important to consider when it comes to looking at how the narcissist behaves. When it comes right down to it, the narcissist is someone that will be controlling. You are likely to see the following behaviors come into play when you are dealing with the narcissist, and they can help you to identify the truth—that the narcissist is destructive, problematic, and really not someone that you want to be around long-term.

Now, let's consider those common behavioral traits that you are likely to encounter.

- **He is critical:** The narcissist always has something to say—and it is rarely ever actually pleasant. This has less to do with you and everything to do with the fact that he is desperately obsessed with power and perfection. He would sooner tell everyone around him that there is a problem with something that they are doing than admit that his standards are impossible—he will simply say that it's not his fault that you can't meet his expectations. Nothing is ever good enough—short of impossible perfection, he will never be satisfied, and therefore, the criticisms will be present.

- **He is always the devil's advocate—even when you don't want him to:** The narcissist likes to poke and prove people wrong. It makes him feel grandiose—he thrives off of proving to himself that he is the best, and this is no exception. To prove the truth to everyone, he will make it a point to take strange stances on topics just to tell you that you are wrong—even when it is a stretch to make the argument that he has chosen in the first place. For example, imagine that you are happy that you have just been offered a great job that you are looking forward to. He may be quick to point out all of the problems with the job that you got to try to make you feel like it isn't as good as you may have initially thought.

- **Malignantly sarcastic:** The narcissist is usually quite sarcastic—even malignantly so. He enjoys knocking people down a few pegs, and he does so with malignant sarcasm. This is when he tells you something, only to tell you that you are overreacting to a joke when you tell him off for it. Imagine that he asks you if you are pregnant as he pokes your stomach. When you get offended, he might laugh it off and say it's not his fault you have a food baby and to stop getting so offended—he was only joking anyway. This kind of sarcasm is done intentionally to inflict pain and annoyance. He wants to make you feel bad about yourself so that he can feel better about himself.

- **Verbally abusive:** Narcissists love verbal abuse. They typically prefer this type over others—especially in person because no evidence can be used after the fact. They love plausible deniability and will use it well to ensure that you can't weaponize the words that he is using against him. He will make it clear that the real nature of the problem is not him, but you and that you must be willing to take responsibility for it. He will call you names. He will berate you. He will do whatever he can to try to degrade you, and ultimately, your identity, in hopes that doing so will sort of fix his problems.

- **Guilt trips often:** Along with the verbal abuse, narcissists favor guilt trips as well. They tend to prey on naturally empathetic people; the exact opposite of what they are and guilt trips are usually highly effective on them when they do so.

- **Gaining control:** The narcissist must be in control of everything at all times, and if he isn't, he won't participate, or at the very least, he will make his participation minimal. He does this to work better for himself; he wants to influence himself into being able to control everything around him because he is superior, at least in his mind. By being superior, he can take control, to influence everything, and maintain his power, and that is a huge ego stroke to him.

Echoism: Narcissistic Abuse Syndrome

When you have been stuck under the thumb of a narcissist for too long, what usually happens is that you start to erode yourself. You start to feel like the world that you lived in was a lie. You start to doubt the truth—you wonder if you were overreacting all along. You effectively get so bogged down with the abuse that you just stop fighting it. To fight it is futile—it is easier just to sit back and let it happen.

When you have suffered at the hands of a narcissist's abuse, abuse that is highly tailored to the narcissist's standards, laden with manipulation, and attempts to keep you down, you run into a very serious problem. It can be hard to pull yourself out of that abuse after so long, but to do so is imperative. Narcissists love to break down people. They erode them over time, molding them into what they want the other person to be. To the narcissist, the other people in his life are nothing more than just tools that can be used, manipulated, and tossed away when they are no longer useful. However, to the person being abused, that is highly hurtful.

It is possible that through being treated in these manners, you start to feel worse about yourself. You can suffer from narcissistic abuse syndrome— a condition in which you have begun to suffer after a significant amount of time spent near or with a narcissist. If you've been exposed to a narcissist for any extended amount of time, perhaps a narcissistic ex or parent, you may already be exhibiting these symptoms. You might not think so at first, but let's go over the most telltale signs that something is wrong and that something will need to be changed to protect yourself and to keep yourself safe.

People suffering from narcissistic abuse syndrome typically have many of the signs of emotional abuse that we have already gone over in this book so far. However, usually for them, the reality is hard to identify. Bogged down by gaslighting, abuse, threats, and so much belittling and demeaning that they no longer know which way is up or down, many of these people simply are complacent in their lives. They don't bother trying to do anything but placate the narcissist, forgetting about their own needs that still must be met as well. The most common signs that someone is suffering from this disorder include:

- **Feeling insane or like they can't trust themselves:** The narcissist's victim often has a hard time figuring out what is true and what isn't, especially when it comes to their perceptions of the world around them. They tend to err on the side of doubting themselves rather than attempting to make themselves feel trusted or secure in themselves.

- **Feeling like they can't trust others:** After all of the abuse endured, they have a hard time thinking that other people won't abuse them the same way and typically just withdraw away, no longer wanting to engage. They don't feel that they can trust anyone else.

- **Feeling a sense of loyalty to the narcissist:** Often, the victim, will defend the narcissist vehemently, saying that it isn't all bad or that the narcissist didn't ruin everything, or that the narcissist isn't responsible for all of the abuse. They often believe that the only person that has ever given them the time of day was the narcissist, and they typically end up feeling indebted because of this.

- **They become submissive:** Even people who were once highly determined to only do what they wanted to so become broken down after the abuse. They usually end up doing whatever they are asked, even when they don't want to. They stop worrying about what they want and instead put all of the emphasis on the narcissist.

Malignant Narcissism and Sociopathy

While most narcissists are just opportunistic, waiting for a time to strike and get what they want, there is a rarer type of narcissism that is quite dangerous. In particular, malignant narcissism is not common, and it is not diagnosed on its own as its distinctive clinical diagnosis. Still, it is recognized by many psychologists as a specific manifestation of narcissism that is quite dangerous. This particular form of narcissism usually carries with it a combination of characteristics, such as:

- Having a prevailing diagnosis of NPD already

- Antisocial behaviors and tendencies

- Aggression, and sometimes even sadism toward other people, or oneself

- Paranoia

This kind of narcissism presents in all sorts of different ways, but the most common point to remember is that malignantly narcissistic people usually just want to inflict harm. They enjoy watching people get hurt. Instead of being indifferent toward the pain, they go out of the way to inflict it in other people for their enjoyment, which is what makes them so dangerous compared to your normal, run of the mill, only in it to opportunistically get his way narcissist.

Often, this kind of narcissist is referred to as a sociopath, especially casually, but the truth is that the malignant narcissist isn't quite the same as sociopathy. The fact that the narcissist tends to get aggressive shows that they are not quite the same.

Handling the Narcissist

When it comes to coping with the narcissist, you have a few key points to consider. It is not impossible to manage, but the truth is, the best way that you can deal with a narcissist is to simply not engage at all. You need to entirely break away from the narcissist so that you can begin to heal and ensure that at the end of the day, you are as healthy as possible. However, that is not always an easy option. If you need to deal with the narcissist on your own, there are several different ways that you can do this that aren't as straight to the point. You can work to avoid the narcissist in other ways, mitigating the damage when you have on other choices but to continue to engage.

Grey rock

The grey rock method is perhaps one of the most effective if you have no choice but to continue to engage with the narcissist. When you engage with the narcissist, you create openings for manipulation and abuse. However, you can learn to overcome that entirely—you can work to ensure that ultimately, the way that you can get along the best is through being able to change up what you are doing and responding.

If the narcissist thrives on you giving an emotional response, the natural result then is to just not give them any emotional responses at all. Channel your inner grey rock—aptly named because you are meant to make yourself as boring and as forgettable as a grey rock that you might pass on your walk. Think about the last time that you went walking—do you remember looking at any of the rocks? Chances are, you don't—because you don't care to remember boring, mundane details that don't matter very much in the grand scheme of things. If you want to be successful in fending off the narcissist, then the best thing that you can do is be boring.

If he talks to you, give him as short of an answer as possible. Turn it into a game—how few words do I need to use to get the point across? What can I do to make myself even more boring and less remarkable now than before?

When you do this, he will lose interest rapidly—why would he bother engaging with you when he doesn't see the point in doing so in the first place?

Set boundaries and stick to them

Your boundaries matter, and the sooner that you can create and stick to them, the more likely that you are to avoid running into problems later on. When you can set a boundary, you must also make sure that you add a consequence as well. This means that you need to make it clear that you are not willing to engage with the narcissist if he can't respect them. If he violates your boundary, you disengage and walk away. It's that simple. After a few times of realizing that he can't just bulldoze over your boundaries without consequence, he will usually lose interest and move on with his life.

Chapter 5: Understanding Neuro-Linguistic Programming

Neuro-linguistic programming, often shortened to just NLP, is a technique that was designed to create a way for ordinary people without any experience in psychology to begin tapping into their minds. It granted them the ability to influence and control the way that they engage with themselves. This is in hopes of being able to then influence and control how they engage with everyone else as well. To do this effectively, you must learn to look at the unconscious mind of the individual that you are interested in understanding. Whether using NLP for yourself or using it to influence other people around you, this tool is highly valuable and is one that you should make sure that you use in your life.

Within this chapter, we are going to look at four key factors—what NLP is, how it works, how it works as a form of manipulation, and how rapport matters. Each point will give you a general understanding of what to expect, how to expect it, and how to ensure that at the end of the day, you can use it all. NLP is a highly powerful tool that utilizes the fact that we don't usually pay attention to the unconscious mind. We rarely acknowledge the truth—that you can alter your behaviors, and the behaviors of those around you—in one very simple way—all you have to do is make it a point to engage with them in a certain manner.

A Look at NLP

NLP is the acknowledgment that, while you don't control much in this world, you do control the thought processes that you have at any point in time. You can't necessarily control how you get through life, and you can't always influence what will happen next to you, but you can make sure that you can control how it hurts you. You can learn how you can better yourself through learning to take control of the thoughts that you have at any point in time.

Effectively, the idea is that you can't control your experience, but you can control the perception.

This works strongly in your favor for one very real reason: Thoughts influence behaviors, and those behaviors influence feelings. Effectively, you experience something in your life. You then have your thoughts about that thing that you have experienced. You must be able to identify those thoughts, and then compound upon it. You need to be able to change up how you engage with your thoughts, and as a result, you can stop yourself from feeling so bad.

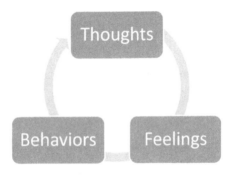

Let's take a look at this in closer depth for a moment. Imagine that you are deathly terrified of birds. Now, most people think that is a little bit strange, but you remember being a kid and having a bird steal your ice cream off of your ice cream cone when you were walking along the beach. When that happened, your fear began. You might not realize that that is the origin story of your phobia, but it is there, weighing on you and keeping you down unless you come up with some way that you can defeat it. The truth is, you have one simple way to do so: You rewrite your perception.

Now, this doesn't mean that you are going to tell yourself that it never happened—rather, you are going to reframe your thoughts. Often, you will find that manipulators do this well. They will make it a point to change up how you experienced something in hopes of that new perception confusing you or convincing you that they are right. When they put their perception into your mind, then you end up engaging with the world from that new viewpoint. It changes your feelings and then your behaviors. This is fundamentally rooted in NLP.

Back to our point now—if you look at your fear of birds, you know that in reality, it stems from one traumatic, and admittedly, pretty comical event as a child that then framed your whole life. Now, as an adult, you can't be around chickens. You refuse to eat turkey dinner for Thanksgiving and instead take the time to avoid any family that isn't willing to prepare ham instead. You are simply terrified of birds, living and dead, and that can be pretty overwhelming in a world where chicken and turkey are both very common protein sources, and birds fly around everywhere that you go.

You know that the event happened, and you perceived it as trauma. From that trauma, you know that you are now afraid of birds—you feel afraid every time that you see one. As a result, you avoid any situations that may involve birds for fear of being stuck with or near one. Those actions that you take to avoid birds, then, make it worse. When you are constantly trying to get away from the birds around you, you just reaffirm that fear of them in the first place. You continue to be afraid of them, and the cycle continues.

With NLP, however, you can disrupt that. More specifically, you can change your perception. You see, the one thing in this world that you can control is your mindset. You are in complete control of your thoughts, even if that control is something that you have given over to someone else. This means, then, that you have an easy fix there. All you have to do to fix the problem is to make sure that you are taking the time to change up how you engage with your fear in the first place.

If you change the frame around how you see birds, instead of seeing that battle between yourself and the seagull over your ice cream cone, you can change it all up—you can instead tell yourself that things weren't as bad as you are making them out to be. You can tell yourself that you are wrong, that you are silly or over-reacting, and as a direct result, you end up feeling differently about the situation. You can instead tell yourself that the great ice cream debacle was funny. After all, how many kids can say that their ice cream was stolen by a bird? And, even better—you got an even bigger ice cream cone after your first one was stolen.

When you start to put yourself through these other thoughts instead, you remind yourself that the truth is, you don't have to be afraid. Over time, you might start to associate birds with humor because of the comedy of the situation, and then, you stop feeling like you have to react so strongly to the birds whenever they are around you.

When you do this enough, you effectively just rewrite your thought processes. You hijack those thoughts that you have that usually influence you to act in certain ways, and you take advantage to ensure that everything else that follows gets a different reaction too. When you do this enough, you get to effectively just reset your thoughts so that you can maintain that complete control over yourself.

Using NLP to Manipulate

As you can see, NLP is highly potent. You can use it to influence yourself to believe new thoughts that can change up your behaviors. However, in the wrong hands, someone can do something very similar to people around them as well. Manipulators can use these techniques with ease to not just influence your thoughts but to control you as well. When you face this, you discover that ultimately, the problem lies not with the methods themselves, but rather, through the user. Manipulation itself, and being able to influence and alter how other people see and think about you, is not inherently dangerous or wrong. It is not inherently a problem for you to be able to influence your mind, or even the minds of others—however, the intentions matter.

Yes, with NLP, you could break someone down. You could work to break their very self-esteem and confidence that make them who they are. You could create new thoughts for them that become the manner through which they address everything. You could make it a point to engage with other people in ways that are hurtful or harmful, or you could engage with them to make them better. Think about it—how often do you see professionals intentionally altering the thoughts of other people? They approach people differently. Think about therapists for a moment—or even NLP practitioners.

NLP was designed so that people could alter thoughts but in a therapeutic process. It was created to create those alterations, and because of that, it is highly potent and highly effective. Ultimately, the best way to ensure that you can do better, then, is to make sure that you know better. Make sure that you are aware of what you are doing so that you can prevent it from hurting other people. If you are going to use NLP, be mindful of the power that you have.

If you are worried about other people manipulating you, be aware of the power that NLP has. With that knowledge, regularly consider whether the reason that you are doing something is that you want to do so, or if you are just engaging because you feel like you have to. When you get better at understanding the nuances between these, you will be able to defend yourself better. You will even be able to use NLP on your own to influence yourself as well, and there would be no problems with you doing that.

Rapport

Ultimately, NLP is built upon rapport—the ability to relate to each other. To have a rapport with someone else is to have a connection with them—it is a sort of camaraderie that you see between friends that makes our minds even more connected than we are probably aware of. Have you ever been to a restaurant and decide to watch people? If you've never done it before, try it—look for a couple that looks like they've been together for a long while. What do you notice about how they move?

Most of the time, as our relationships build, we create rapport with each other. We create this ability to understand each other at a deeper level, and this is usually shown by taking a look at how we move around each other. People who have a solid rapport with each other usually tend to move at the same time. They mirror each other—this process shows that they are connected closely. You will usually breathe, walk, eat, and drink at the same pace as your friend if you are together. You will naturally synchronize your steps together. You will stand in the same poses. You will probably also do other things together at the same time. This is because, when you like someone else, your mind sort of synchronizes with them. It is a part of our nonverbal communication. We see our friend doing something, and unconsciously, we shift to do the same thing. This is natural; we do it because we want to make sure that we are constantly in the same positions as those around us. We crave to be liked; we crave to be connected to people, and ultimately, the way that we achieve that likeness, that sense f belonging, is to mimic each other.

Rapport is also the key to NLP. If you don't have a good rapport with someone else, you probably won't be able to connect clearly with them. You probably won't be able to ensure that you are working well with them or altering their mind. You need to create that connection somehow. This is done primarily through mirroring, a process that will involve you effectively tricking the creation of that apport. You force the point by mimicking the other person first. When you can do that, you essentially just fool their minds into doing the same back to you. You teach them that they should be mirroring you back, so they do, and as a result, you end up creating that confidence between each other.

With the rapport built through mirroring, you can then begin to tap into the other person's subconscious mind with your movements and actions. You can make it a point to change up how you move and act so that you can take control. This is done quite simply, all things considered—it just takes four simple steps:

1. **Listen actively:** Start by giving the other person your entire attention. Look at them in the eyes, listen to them and nod your head as you do—three times is the perfect amount. When you use the triple nod, as it is often referred to, you tell them that you are listening, understanding, and agreeing with them. Keep your body language open at this time and make it a point to engage carefully and openly with them. Feel that

you have that connection and believe in it. The belief is what helps.

2. **Mimic them:** Next comes shifting over to starting to mimic or mirror the other person. You do this carefully. However, if you aren't careful, you can just tip them off that you are doing it—and that can cause new problems. Instead of letting them think that you are following along ad overtly copying them, latch onto something else instead. It is often recommended that you try to match your voice to theirs—make sure that you keep their pitch, their speed, and their excitement. If you can do this, you will start to follow along with them, and their mind will catch onto this as well—unconsciously, they will sense that you are following along, and they will start building up that rapport.

3. **Find their signature:** Every person has their signature when they talk. It is something that is done for emphasis over

the conversation. Some people have something physical—they may move in a certain way. Others may have something verbal, such as saying something that shows that they have made their point, kind of like a catchphrase. Figure out what the other person's is so that you can make good use of it. You need to know what theirs is so that you can take full advantage of the ability to create that rapport for yourself. When you have identified it, watch to see when you think that they are getting ready to use it—and then beat them to using it. They will be thrilled that you seem to be on the same page as them, and you will start up that rapport.

4. **Test it:** Finally, the last thing for you to do is test the situation. The best way to test it is to make some small, innocuous motion and see if the other person follows along. If they do, you were probably successful. If not, you might want to try again.

Chapter 6: Hypnosis

Now, if someone told you that they could hypnotize you and make you walk around and pretend to be a pig, would you believe them? Most people wouldn't—after all, the power of our minds is too strong for such nonsense, isn't it? The truth is, however, that isn't the case at all. When it comes right down to it, we are easily influenced during hypnosis- but the catch is, we have to be open and receptive to it in the first place for it to be effective at all. When it comes down to it, hypnosis is powerful—it can be used to influence other people, but it is also difficult to use if you don't know what you are doing and if you don't know how to trigger someone else to get into that relaxed state. It is one of those things that will require you to be able to get someone else into a state of extreme relaxation and suggestibility. When you can do that, you can start to influence them and how they work.

Within this chapter, we will address what hypnosis is and how it works to influence the minds of those around you. We will also look at the most common forms of hypnosis, as well as take a look at how

NLP and hypnosis go hand in hand. The truth is, they are both quite similar to each other, and the sooner that you can recognize that truth, the better.

What Is Hypnosis?

First, let's consider one point—hypnosis is NOT coercive. It is not something that can be forced upon someone else at all. It is something that must be carefully fostered and encouraged over time—to hypnotize someone else requires you to be able to encourage them to see things your way. To hypnotize someone else is to make them want to open up their minds to you somehow. It is collaborative.

Where it becomes the case of manipulation happening is when you have a manipulator who understands how hypnosis works, and they go through the time and effort to convince someone else to do something for them. However, it is not a quick effort—it takes time to get it to happen. Rapport has to be built. They have to be convinced and suggested to behave in these ways. They have to want to do so—if the person under hypnosis is not willing to do something, they simply won't do it. They have to be willing.

Effectively, there is a sort of "implied contract" between the person under hypnosis and the one doing the hypnotizing in the first place. This does, of course, mean that the other person could take advantage. This does mean that it is possible to use hypnosis in a way that is going to influence and control people for the negative, but by and large, hypnosis itself is not a bad thing. Again, we are right back to the idea of is it the tool that is the problem, or is it the person wielding the tool?

How Hypnosis Works

Hypnosis work because, ultimately, the person being hypnotized wants to be suggested to. It is a state in which the hypnotist carefully guides them through their mind, working to slowly but surely help them figure out what it is that they want. When you can understand this, you start to see hypnosis for what it is—really just a way for two people to work together to make something happen. When you learn to do this effectively, you can usually get the other person to achieve great things. For example, hypnosis is often used to help people do things that they didn't think that they were capable of in the first place. A common one is helping people to lose weight when they want to. When you want to be able to lose weight, you must first be able to convince your mind to do so. Some people struggle with this and, as a direct result, never actually lose weight. However, with hypnosis, you can make it happen.

Hypnosis works because it allows you to later the unconscious thought processes that you are having. Remember how we discussed the fact that NLP worked by exactly that process? Through being able to tell yourself that you need to change your unconscious thoughts and then doing so, you can encourage your mind to do so.

Relaxation Suggestability Change

Imagine this for a moment—you want to lose weight. However, your subconscious mind thinks that you will fail. Maybe you have failed in the past, or maybe you think that you are too weak-willed or otherwise unable to make it happen. No matter the reason, you have this firm belief that you are the problem and that you will not lose weight. So then, what do you think will happen? Naturally, if you don't believe that you will be able to lose weight, you won't be able to. You defeated yourself and set yourself up to fail. As a direct result, you are stuck—you can't change up what you were doing, and you can't figure out how you will be able to prevent that problem in the future.

However, with hypnosis, you get in there and change those subconscious and unconscious thoughts. Instead of being able to tell yourself that you are never going to lose the weight, you can remind yourself that you can lose the weight—you just have to be diligent enough to make it happen.

You can fix that problem, and in doing so, you can tell yourself that you actually can do better—you actually can lose that weight.

With your subconscious mind now redirected in a new direction, you know that you will be able to better trust yourself and your thoughts. You will be able to make sure that you take the time to lose weight at that time because your mind will believe that you can do so in the first place.

As you can see, then, hypnosis and NLP are more or less the same—you are using a partnership between two people to alter the thought processes to change up the behaviors as well. When you do that, you know that you are able to change up behaviors with ease. Both NLP and hypnosis are potent forms of being able to influence the mind, used in different manners, to get to the same end goal.

Common Forms of Hypnosis

Now, let's take a look at some of the most common ways that hypnosis can occur. Like NLP, there are many different options out there. There are four distinct types that we will go over now.

Traditional hypnosis

First, we will consider the traditional hypnosis. This is the most basic form that is able to work because of the simplicity. It is designed to rely on very little—you just work to create a hypnotic state, usually through the process of listening to something or speaking slowly, deliberately, and at a very constant pace without changing much up. When you do this, you are usually able to enter that state of extreme suggestibility in which you can start to put in those new thoughts that you want. When you are in that relaxed state, those new thoughts are said to you, installed, and reinforced. Then, your mind tends to just absorb those thoughts, taking them on, and making good use of them on its own. As a direct result, you end up changing thoughts and being able to fix how you think and engage. With your thoughts changed, you can then see the behaviors change as well.

Ericksonian hypnosis

Next, let's look at Ericksonian hypnosis. This kind, based on the practices of Dr. Milton Erickson, is designed to work through metaphor. This is done because often, when people are skeptical of hypnosis, they resist it. However, this allows you to get around it. The metaphors will naturally compare and contrast things in order to begin to encourage the desired behaviors. The mind, through the metaphors, therefore gets to the point of understanding the thoughts that you wanted to install in the first place. This is done with isomorphic metaphors—those that draw one on one comparisons between a moral of a story and a problem that is being faced by the mind. Additionally, it can be done with interspersal metaphors, which are designed to embed the commands that you want to use, allowing them to avoid detection in the first place.

NLP hypnosis

NLP hypnosis is a form that is commonly used with NLP techniques. Techniques such as anchoring, reframing, and flashing are used to help to overcome problematic thoughts to create the behaviors that you actually want to be exhibiting in the first place. They are done effectively, and they can be performed individually through self-hypnosis, or with the help of someone else instead.

Self-hypnosis

Finally, let's consider self-hypnosis. This form is done individually, allowing yourself to learn to put yourself into a deep trance that you can then use, encouraging yourself to enter that state of relaxation so that you are able to then suggest to yourself what you want to do, or you can even have a sound clip that offers the suggestions instead. It can be done entirely independently.

Chapter 7: Deception

Now, let's take some time to consider deception. The act of deception is to be able to obscure the truth. It is used to hide behind for some reason or to make sure that you are able to obscure something. However, the topic of what is deception can be somewhat vague for some people. What is considered deception, and what is ignorance? Is a white lie a form of deception? Is there ever a point in time where deception is actually a good thing to use? These are all fantastic questions and are highly relevant in consideration of dark psychology, manipulation, and narcissistic abuse. Within this chapter, we are going to stop and define what deception is. We will take a look at whether it is inherently evil or a problem, and we will also address how to spot it out and about so that you can know for sure when you are exposed to it so that you can protect yourself and keep yourself safe.

Defining Deception

Deception itself is defined as the action of deceiving someone. It is to inherently cover up something; to try to cause someone else to accept something that is inherently false or wrong as valid. It is effectively a trick or a scam—it is something that can be used to alter your understanding of something, or to fool you into doing something that is deemed a scam or a trick.

Ultimately, deception has one purpose: It is there to conceal something. It is intended to be a way that you or someone else is able to completely mislead someone else in hopes of being able to obscure the truth. Maybe you did something that you don't want other people to know about. Maybe you want to know if you can get out of trouble by pretending that you haven't done anything. At all, or maybe you want to steal credit for something. No matter the reason that you want to deceive someone, the truth is, if you aren't careful, people will discover the truth. They will realize that there was a lie.

Typically, deception involves a position of trust, which you can leverage to be able to directly alter the way that you engage with someone else. It could be that you do so because you are trying to offer some sort of sympathy and protection—you may tell your child that the dog went off to play on a farm or that the cat ran away from home instead of telling your child the truth—that your beloved household pet has died. Now, at some point, your child will probably learn the truth—they will most likely notice at some point that ultimately, you had told them something else, and they will probably be annoyed, roll their eyes, and move on with life.

Other people, however, are different. When you deceive other people, you are eroding that trust in them. If you cheat on a partner, for example, there is a good chance that you will deal with backlash somewhere. Likewise, if you lie about something at work, or pretend that you have credentials that you don't, you may run into new problems. While people will initially believe you, there is also a good chance that they will also begin to see the truth— that you were lying to them and that you have directly deceived them about something potentially serious.

That trust, when you damage it to such a degree, cannot be easily earned back. It takes time and effort to get everyone interested in believing you after you have deceived them and that means that you will have to take the time to ensure that you are able to better

Deception is, inherently, dark just by virtue of what you are doing. You are really just lying or attempting to lie without making it clear that you are doing so. To lie to other people is inherently wrong, and for that reason, it is important to understand how deception works and how to spot it when someone else is lying to you. When you are able to spot these differences, you will be able to do so much better; you will learn what it will take to notice when someone else is lying to you so that you can avoid it from being a bigger problem later on. You can prevent yourself from falling for lies and other forms of deception just by virtue of understanding what goes into doing so.

Forms of Deception

Deception is as flexible as we make it; it is able to be changed up with ease just by virtue of the fact that it wields words as its language. We have an indefinite amount of words that we can use at the end of the day, and because of that, it is very easy to create an endless list of ways that you can lie to each other. However, no matter what the lie itself is, let's take a look at how they can be formatted. It will almost always follow one of several patterns.

Lies

These are the most basic forms of deception—they occur when you are telling something that is not actually true. When you lie to someone else, you tell them that one thing is the truth, when in reality, what you are saying is entirely wrong. This differs from just exaggerating one way or another—it is more than that. It is trying to convince someone else that 2+2=6 and expect them to be perfectly okay with it. To lie to someone else involves you simply not telling people about what the truth is. Whether you lie about whether you were involved in something, you say that you don't know what happened to something that was in your possession at the time of becoming damaged or otherwise obscure the real truth, the fact of the matter is that you have lied. It is specifically attempting to cover something up, and that is the problem.

Equivocations

Equivocations refer to veiling the truth behind ambiguity. You are deliberately wording things in a way that could be taken in either context in hopes of being able to hide the truth—you hope that because you answered it so that any option is technically true, to some degree, by what you have said, that no one can argue. Think of the expertise of politicians here—they are skilled at saying things in just the right way that will work to appeal to everyone involved. You are trying to answer with a vague answer that doesn't quite answer the initial question but obscures everything just enough to be passable.

Effectively, when you do this, you deceive just by virtue of the fact that you are intentionally obscuring the truth. You aren't upfront about what you have done, or you are trying to otherwise hide what you are doing or thinking, and as such, you run into all sorts of new problems and technicalities. For example, consider what would happen if you slapped a label onto something that said that it was made in the USA. In reality, the *label* was made in the USA, but the actual product had been outsourced. This kind of equivocation is meant to effectively mislead people so that they can be pacified, and you can move on.

Concealment

Some people prefer to simply conceal the truth. Making use of concealment involves intentionally leaving out information in hopes of it going completely missed. You might leave out details that might reflect poorly on you, for example. Imagine that you and someone else got into an altercation. The police come to question the two of you to calm things down. You say that you were defending yourself because the other person did something first. Never mind the fact that in reality, you had been harassing the other person prior to that incident. When you leave out details, you are effectively hoping that the other person doesn't realize the truth—that you may have actually been more involved than you are letting on.

Exaggerations

Another common form of deception is to exaggerate something. When you exaggerate the value of something, for example, you make the other person think that they are getting one value when, in reality, you are deceiving them. This is done for on every specific reason—you do so because you hope that you will be able to entice someone into doing something, knowing full well that you are deceptive about it.

For example, imagine that you need an excuse for why you can't work one day because you were up drinking the night before, and you are feeling a bit hungover. You text your boss, letting him know that you are sick and vomiting and that you can't work because you don't want to get anyone else sick. Now, you are sick—but hangovers are not contagious. Hangovers are caused by your own actions, not by something that can be passed on to other people. However, when you exaggerate, you are making something sound worse; you can usually get what you wanted without too much hassle or pushback.

Understatements

When you make an understatement, you do the exact opposite. Instead of telling something and making it worse, you try to downplay it. Perhaps you dropped someone's phone and shattered the screen. Instead of apologizing profusely and offering to fix the problem, you shrug it off. "Oh, it's barely scratched!" you may tell the other person, "It'll be just fine. You can barely tell, and you can still use it anyway. Why are you complaining?" By doing this, you attempt to obscure the truth by making it not as big of a deal as it actually is. Then, when anyone asks you what happened, later on, you might shrug and say that the other person made a big fuss over a little scratch.

Spotting Deception

If you want to spot deception, you have plenty of methods that you can use that will help you to do so. Once you know what you are doing, you will be able to do so with ease. You just have to know where to start and what the common behavioral cluster giveaways are. The truth is, we are very readable. As a species, humans are able to be read quite simply when people know what to look for. Let's go over how to tell when you are being lied to now.

Know the stress signs

Start by familiarizing yourself with the common stress signs. These are what tell you that there is probably something going on that is making the other person uncomfortable. The truth is, most people don't like lying. They don't like being deceptive about something, and when they have to, their bodies usually betray what has happened. The most common stress signs that you will notice when lying include:

- **An increased pace of breathing:** While you can't easily see someone else's pulse or blood pressure when you are looking at them, you can see how they are breathing, and oftentimes, the unconscious mind will naturally quicken the breath of someone being deceptive. This is because of the fact that your body is under stress. As your heart quickens, so does your breathing.

- **Closed body language:** Usually, you will see that the other person is going to be very closed off after lying as well—they will, for example, cross off their arms and keep their bodies folded inward.

- **The freeze response:** If you ask a question that they are not prepared to answer honestly, you may find that they tell you that they are not actually truthful. They would freeze up when they are mid-lie or just before telling anyone anything.

- **Avoiding eye contact:** Refusing to make eye contact is another sign that there's something up and that the other person may be being deceptive because they don't want to lie, whether they admit it to themselves or not.

- **Staring:** Sometimes, you will find that the liar will actually just stare instead of looking away. This is because so many people know that they are supposed to be making eye contact to avoid detection for lying, so they try to overcompensate for the desire to look away, but in doing so, they end up becoming more obvious about their lying.

- **The lying cluster:** When lying, there is one particular cluster of behaviors that are seen pretty frequently—it is touching the hand, the face, crossing the arms together, and leaning back. When this happens, you know that you are probably being lied to. Pay attention to these particular behaviors to protect yourself from being deceived.

- **The words:** There are very specific patterns that you will catch when you are being lied to. Usually, you will be deflected when you are lied to. The deceiver will typically deflect regularly—they will make it a point to avoid directly answering. For example, if you ask someone if they broke something, they might tell you, "What am I, 5?" Did they answer the question? Not directly—but they implied that they were not responsible, despite quite possibly bearing that responsibility.

You will want to look at all of these different signs, figuring out whether they are genuinely presented to you or if they just happen to be part of the other party's general body language tendencies in the first place.

Chapter 8: Understanding Brainwashing

Brainwashing is a particular form of manipulation or control over someone else that is used through very specific means—usually, when you use brainwashing, you are referring to a very specific pattern that is used typically in hostage situations to try to get the other person to give in to control. Brainwashing most often occurs in the context of trying to get someone else to conform to something new.

The purpose of brainwashing comes right down to thought reform—when it is used, the entire purpose is to get compliance and reeducation to encourage someone to become someone that they are not. Within this chapter, we are going to define brainwashing, as well as get into how it works. We will also take a look at the most common steps to going through the process.

Defining Brainwashing

Perhaps the first reported source of brainwashing was recorded during the Korean War. During this time, it is reported that several American prisoners of war were held in prison camps and were brainwashed into believing that they had engaged in germ warfare as well as pledged allegiance to communism. During the time that this happened, they were effectively stripped of their identities, forced to comply, and denounced everything that they had known of their past lives. They had their thoughts literally rewritten through coercion and threat.

Brainwashing ultimately is a form of influence that is designed to be invasive and forceful to break down the other person's mind. They eventually comply in hopes of protecting themselves from being hurt worse. It becomes self-preservation to do whatever they are told to do to protect themselves, and as a result, they are willing to take on complex personas that are entirely dictated by the captors.

The Science of Brainwashing

Brainwashing is believed to work because the agent, that is to say, the person doing the brainwashing, is gaining complete and utter control over the target, the person that is being brainwashed in the first place. This makes it so that the agent has complete power over everything and anything related to the individual. The agent gets to determine when needs can be met and how they are. Over time, the end result is a systematic destruction of everything that goes into making that person who they are. Over time, because they can't meet their needs, they feel like their identities are destroyed to the point of no longer being viable. Over time, through torture, coercion, and control, brainwashing can occur. Typically, however, it should be noted that over time, the individual's old identity can be returned. After leaving the dangerous situation, it is possible, with therapy, for the old identity to be returned.

Using Brainwashing

When brainwashing happens, it is usually done through several steps that are designed to be as effective as possible. These steps are brutal, but that is the entire purpose of it all. It is designed to be brutal so that it can have its intended effect. Let's go over the steps that go into this method now.

1. **Assault on identity:** The first step is designed to help to break down the self. It is an assault on your direct identity. It is designed to make you feel like you are not

who you are. Typically, in the actual context, the agent will deny everything. They will directly contradict anything that the individual may say is true. As this happens, the individual is under attack repeatedly to the point of exhaustion and eventually, even giving in to what the other person said.

2. **Guilt:** Next, the individual has to be made to feel guilty. This is done so that the individual is more likely to give up his or her identity. When that entire identity is all wrapped up in guilt, it is easier to get rid of it and pretend that it is not there than it is to do anything else. By rejecting the identity entirely, the individual is even closer to being brainwashed.

3. **Self-betrayal:** Next comes the stage in which the agent gets the target to agree with what has been said. The agent wants the target to recognize that he or she is bad and that it is time to denounce who they once were. They need to feel like they were

wrong to have the opinions that they did so that they are able to do better.

4. **Breaking point:** That betrayal culminates in what is known as the breaking point—the point at which the individual just cannot cope any longer. At this point, the target goes through what is commonly referred to as a nervous breakdown—sobbing, depression, and generally just not coping well. They may be in the middle of a psychotic episode or may have other problems going on as well. They believe that all hope is lost, and that is the key to the whole process.

5. **Leniency:** When all seems beyond help, that is when the agent can get in and take control. Usually, with a small kindness— offering a bit of leniency or otherwise offering a drink of water, and that small kindness is enough to make the individual feel indebted.

6. **The compulsion to confess:** At this point, the target realizes that they have

hope. All is not lost, and they can do what it will take to protect themselves. So, what they do is they confess. They want to try to channel and relieve their stress and guilt, so they confess.

7. **Channeling the guilt:** At this point, the target assumes that he or she is just wrong. The target assumes that they are wrong for some reason, and they want to get rid of that sense—which gets connected to their guilt. They wrap all of their guilt about their identity together to release it.

8. **Releasing the guilt:** The target realizes the problem is not with him or her, but rather, with the guilt and beliefs. They do not have to be permanently bad or problematic—they can get better and do better to release the pain and escape. So, they do this through confessions.

9. **Progress toward harmony:** At this point, the target is able to begin making a move toward what they perceive as salvation or goodness—they can rebuild

themselves to be good, and in doing so, in deciding to assimilate and comply, they are able to make the abuse stop. In denouncing the past, the target is able to begin choosing the new belief system, making a conscious choice to assimilate and comply. As a result, he or she comes to the conclusion that this new identity is reliable and safe, and they follow it.

10. **Final confession:** Finally, the new life is clung to. All old beliefs are rejected, and the individual pledges allegiance to the new life instead. This typically involves

Chapter 9: Speed Reading to Understand People

If you are ready to read other people, then this is the chapter for you. Ultimately, being able to read other people is highly important. If you want to be able to understand what is going on in someone else's mind, you need to be able to tell what is going on with their bodies first. The truth is, people are quite easy to learn to read if you know what you are doing. All you have to do is make sure that you are looking at certain clusters.

Ultimately, we all communicate with people in different ways. We have both verbal and nonverbal signals that we give off at all times. However, the bulk of our communication is nonverbal. We have plenty of body language that we use in all sorts of different ways to be able to understand what is going on with other people. We look at things such as proximity to each other and general demeanor to figure out what is going on inside one person's mind so that we can get more information from them. When you do this, you learn to recognize how you can interpret what they are about to do, if they are going to do anything at all.

Within this chapter, we are going to take a look at what it will take for you to begin understanding other people at a glance. You will learn how to understand the basic expressions, attraction, closed behavior, assertiveness, and dominance. All of these are important in their own ways, serving important roles that you can utilize. All you have to do is make sure that you know what to look for!

Reading Expressions

Ultimately, we have seven primary expressions—these are known as our universal expressions because you can spot them pretty much in any culture. No matter where you are from, you know what a smile is, and you can recognize it immediately. That is because a smile is an expression that is considered universal. Let's look at the six universal emotions now so that you can better see what to expect with them.

Happiness

Happiness is easy to understand. When you see someone that's happy, you can recognize it by the smile primarily. However, the most obvious sign of happiness is the crinkle in the eyes—this is how you know that the smile and happiness are legitimate.

Sadness

When it comes to sadness, you can identify it by the fact that the entire face melts, so to speak. You can see that the eyebrows go down. The corners of the mouth do as well, and the inner corners of the brows go up. There may or may not be crying involved as well.

Anger

Anger is defined by three primary characteristics, aside from the demeanor that goes with it. Usually, someone who is angry will have their brows lowered while pressing their lips together firmly. Alternatively, the mouth may be open, bearing teeth and squared.

Fear

Fear is usually shown as brows up high on the face, but still flat, with the eyes widened. The mouth also usually opens widely as well.

Surprise

Surprise is similar to fear in people, but the marked difference is that the jaw lowers alongside the opening of the mouth, and the eyes are usually opened wider, showing whites on both sides. The brows are also arched instead of just raised.

Disgust

Disgust is noticed primarily by taking a look at how the face comes together. The upper lip goes up, rising slightly. The nose bridge usually wrinkles as well, and the cheeks pinch in and up to try to protect the eyes.

Reading Attraction

When someone is attracted to someone else, they show very obvious body language as well. In particular, you can expect to see all sorts of specific actions. The body does not usually lie, and because of that, you can look directly at the behaviors that someone is doing to figure out if they are attracted to you or not. In particular, you want to look for the following behaviors:

- **Sustained eye contact:** You will see that the other person will maintain eye contact more when they are attracted to you. Additionally, they will usually look away, and then glance right back to see if you're still watching them.

- **Smiling:** there is a reason we assume smiling is flirting—it happens often. The flirty, attracted smile usually lasts longer and includes flirty eye contact as well, fleeting, but regular.

- **Self-grooming:** Men and women both do this—they brush their hair with their hands, adjust their clothes, and otherwise tamper with their appearance when they are flirting or talking to someone they find attractive. If they do this regularly, they may really be attracted to you.

- **Looking nervous:** Being nervous is a very normal thing when attracted to someone else, and this usually shows itself through fiddling with something repeatedly.

- **Leaning in:** Typically, people will lean in toward things that they are attracted to, and people are no exception to that rule. You will also notice that the feet will point at the person that the individual is attracted to.

- **Licking the lips:** This is a common one, but it is subtle and easy to miss. However, you can notice it if you pay close attention. Usually, it is noticeable by a quick part of the lips and a small suck or lick.

Reading Assertiveness

Assertiveness is calm, confident, and in control. Effectively, if someone is assertive, they are behaving as if they are in control—they take charge, they are comfortable with themselves, but also won't really go out of their way to overstep on other people either. They simply sit back and allow things to play out without letting anyone else dominate them. The most common signs of assertiveness include:

- **Smooth body movements:** When you are assertive over something, you don't have jerky movements. They are smooth and in control without much of a problem, even when energized or emotional. The voice sounds smooth as well, and they slowly and steadily look about.

- **Balanced:** The assertive individual is usually upright, relaxed, but also well balanced and comfortable.

- **Open body language:** Usually, these people will show that they are open to engagement without being threatening or provocative. They do not block off their bodies at all and show open hands as well.

- **Eye contact regularly:** Eye contact is usually steady and maintained comfortably without much of a problem.

- **Smiling:** There are plenty of polite smiles and listening well with this body language as well. Usually, you can expect the other person to be quite comfortable, and they will smile easily and appropriately.

- **Firm:** While they are firm, they usually have a solid stance without much of a problem. They are not aggressive at all and usually show that they are willing to listen, but they are also firm. They do not escalate anything and tend to avoid aggression in any form.

Reading Domination

Domination is a little more than assertiveness. Usually, with assertiveness, you see someone that is showing that they are confident without being threatening. However, with dominance, you can expect to see a much more threatening demeanor. A dominating body is going to show signs such as:

- **Facial aggressiveness:** You will be able to see the aggression in the face—usually in the form of frowning and sneering, or even snarling.

- **Staring:** The aggressive individual will usually stare at someone that they don't like, or may also squint or attempt to avoid looking at someone entirely.

- **Wide body stance:** They will usually stand out with their shoulders widened, and may even hold their arms wide open as well. They may also stand with their hands placed firmly on their hips in a crotch display.

- **Sudden movements:** You may notice that the aggressor is very rough with his movements, moving about suddenly and even erratically sometimes. It is a good sign that he or she is not in a very good spot at that moment and may do something else aggressive as well.

- **Large gestures:** You may notice that as the individual moves, he will signal with aggressive, almost too big or wide movements that get close to you without ever getting close enough to touch you.

Reading Closed Behavior

Finally, let's go over closed behavior before we continue. Closed behavior shows that the individual is not interested in engaging with the other party at all. When you see closed behavior, you know that the individual is not going to want to engage with you; you know that you are going to see that they want to be left alone, or that they are not receptive to being interacted with then. You can expect to see signs of this sort of behavior, such as:

- **Crossed arms:** This is perhaps the most telltale sign. When someone is feeling closed off, they will almost always cross their arms and keep their hands near to their body. When they speak during this time, they will keep a monotone voice. Think of this as your sign that you are creating a barrier between yourself and the other party with your arms. You want to be left alone, so you close yourself off entirely.

- **Crossed legs:** You can also cross off legs as well—when you do this, you see that the knees are across from each other when sitting down, or they can also cross the ankles as well. This creates an even more closed off image that shows that you are defensive and not willing to listen or change your viewpoint on something.

- **Looking away:** It is also very common to see that the closed-off person wants nothing to do with those around them. They don't want to look at the person that is engaging with them.

- **Leaning away:** You may also see that the closed-off person wants nothing to do with getting close to the individual that is engaging with them either. Instead, they will pull away and lean back, trying to put as much distance between them as possible.

- **Feet turned away:** Look to the feet when you want to know how engaged someone else is. If you see that the other person is standing away, feet pointing away from you, they are closed off and don't want to engage in the conversation at all.

Chapter 10: Regain Control of Your Life

Now, when it comes to regaining control of your life, you have a few options. You can work to protect yourself from dark psychology and manipulation just by working with yourself. Learning to set your boundaries and defend them is perhaps one of the greatest things that you can do that will allow you to regain control of your life and the sooner that you commit to doing so, the sooner that you can be free of the nonsense that will otherwise threaten to take over.

If you want to make sure that you are safe from being manipulated, then consider this chapter as your guide to doing exactly this. We are going to address first how to help yourself be protected. Then, we will consider how you can positively influence those around you.

Protecting Yourself from Dark Psychology and Manipulation

If you want to be protected against dark psychology and manipulation, then there are a few ways that you can protect yourself. Ultimately, the best way to be defended against harm is to make sure that you just cut yourself off from those around you that are manipulative, but when that can't be done reasonably, you can fight back in other ways. When you want to protect yourself from the manipulation and harassment of dark people, the best way to do so includes the following:

- **Reject the need for approval from others:** This is simple: if you stop letting other people define you, you can step away from needing them to constantly influence you. You can remove that need from approval and disconnect all sorts of strings. Now, this is easier said than done, but ultimately, the best way for you to do this is to make sure that you recognize the truth: The manipulator can only manipulate you if you give him the strings to do so. He knows that you have that need to be needed, and he will use it against you every single time. To do this, consider the following points as well:

○ *Recognize the truth:* See that he is just trying to manipulate you and control you. His affection or attention isn't worth it.

○ *You don't need to change other people:* You really can't make them change anyway. Trying to do so is futile and just a waste of your time.

○ *Don't defend yourself:* You don't owe anyone an explanation most of the time. If you start getting defensive, it is time to break it off and stop trying. Forget trying to defend other people and just work with yourself instead.

• **Protect your boundaries:** Remember that you are allowed to say no. Telling someone no, and even disappointing someone else is not off-limits. You are allowed to insist on things your way if you choose to do so, and there is no reason that you can't tell someone that you don't want to do something. You are within your rights to tell other people when they are crossing your boundaries, and you deserve the respect of having them move away from you as you do so.

- **Stop second-guessing yourself:** Make sure that when you have a gut feeling about something being a certain way, you remember to honor it. Don't tell yourself that you're overreacting if you notice something that isn't quite right. You have those gut reactions for a reason, and you owe it to yourself to honor them. Remember, you are meant to be intuitive. You know when someone is doing something cruel or unfair, and you need to honor that. If you start to doubt yourself, remind yourself that you are worthy of being trusted.

- **Up your emotional intelligence:** Emotional intelligence is your way of being able to understand and empathize with other people. When you are emotionally intelligent, you usually recognize your emotional reactions and tendencies and can understand them. Likewise, you start to better understand what other people are doing, as well. In doing this, you develop a better understanding of what it will keep yourself steady. You will be able to keep yourself calm, and in control, and in doing so, you will discover that you can remain in control of many different situations. You don't have to allow manipulators to take control. You can tell yourself not to fall for it, and you can keep your emotions steady, so that is the case. Emotional intelligence is ultimately developed through self-awareness—you have to be self-aware enough to use it accordingly. If you are, you will be able to successfully navigate all sorts of situations, and you will be able to ensure that you are, ultimately, able to recognize when you are making mistakes so that you can correct them.

Positively Influencing Others with These Skills

When it comes to being able to influence other people, you have plenty of other options as well. You can work, for example, to begin persuading people to do something that will benefit them. You can learn to help other people so that they can feel more confident, happier, and more in charge than they have been in the past, and all it will take from you is making sure that you know how to use your skills for good reasons.

Let's go over some of the ways that you could influence other people with the skills that you learned about reading over this book.

Using NLP to build confidence in others

First, consider the fact that the NLP can be used to help yourself to influence those around you. When you use NLP methods, you can start to insist to your friends or others around you that they are actually worth the confidence that you want them to have. You can talk to them, influencing them to remind them that ultimately, they should feel okay about themselves because people are all deserving of that fact.

You can help those around you begin to understand and change their thought processes as well. Through listening, reframing, and working well with the other person, you can remind them that really, they can control their thought processes to change their behaviors as well. Remember, you are in control of yourself. You can control the way that you change your behaviors as well, and just like you can, so too can those around you. When you make this a priority, you help other people begin to follow those tendencies as well.

Using hypnosis to help others

When you utilize tools like hypnosis, you learn that you can help to carefully and quietly influence people without them being entirely aware of what you are doing. You can soothe them with your voice, using a nice, soft, calm voice to remind them that they are doing okay, and then, you can also inform them of what you think that they need to hear. If they trust you enough to listen to you well, then you will be able to help them see all of the different ways in which you can begin to influence them. You can remind them that they are confident, that they are smart, worthy, and anything else that they need to hear, and they will be happy to hear it. In these hypnotic states, you can usually influence them into feeling better about themselves as well.

Understanding body language to influence others

When you know how other people's body language can be read, you know that you can deescalate situations with ease. When you are worried about how someone is going to interact with you, you know that you will be able to recognize how they are approaching the situation. Because you will be able to tell what is going on with them, you should also be able to change up your interactions in ways that will help problems from arising.

For example, imagine that you see that the other person is feeling quite stressed out as they engage with you. You will know that they are not comfortable and therefore can decide that what you should do is give them some space so that they can relax. By offering that space up to them, you will realize that you can deescalate the problem. You can change up your body language to ensure that, ultimately, you can better engage with those around you without setting anyone else off. This can help you to make sure that you are not unintentionally offending or annoying someone without realizing the effect that you were having in the first place.

Chapter 11: Bonus Tips and Strategies to Combat Dark Tactics

Finally, we have arrived at the end of this book, and before we close it up, let's take some time to consider several strategies to help yourself fight off dark tactics. When you learn to follow these steps, you can protect yourself and ensure that you are in charge.

Don't Apologize Unnecessarily

Start by remembering that you should not apologize if you have nothing to apologize for. Apologizing unnecessarily just gives the other party more control over you that can be used to influence and manipulate you with ease. When you refuse to apologize for something that has nothing to do with you, however, you remove that control. You make it impossible for them to take over what you are doing and hold it against you.

At first, this may seem difficult, but the truth is, if you can keep yourself from apologizing needlessly, you can boost your confidence, among other great benefits that you may not even realize you are missing out on. For example, consider the point that apologizing when unneeded just puts you in an unconsciously submissive or guilty position. You are not at fault, and therefore, you have nothing to feel guilty for. Only apologize when you have genuinely done something wrong and be mindful of how you do so.

Use Affirmations Regularly

Affirmations are great tools for you to use to boost up your self-esteem if necessary. When you use affirmations, you have little statements that you can say to yourself that will help you to remind yourself that you are not as bad, troubled, or problematic as you may think. You do not need to allow yourself to feel bad about yourself. You don't need to tell yourself that you will fail, or that you are unlovable. Affirmations can help you to remind yourself that you are deserving of love and affection as well.

When you use an affirmation, you must consider three key points: Your affirmation must be positive, present tense, and personal. When you can do this, you know that your affirmation will be effective and, therefore, is something that you should be utilizing. For example, perhaps you have a problem with constantly feeling like you are at fault when you have not done anything wrong. You just assume that you are the problem, even when you're not. You may create an affirmation such as, "I am doing my very best every day, and that is good enough for me." A statement like this reminds you that ultimately, you don't have to be as stressed out as you have been. With that kind of statement, you know that you are okay. You remind yourself not to take things so personally and that you are okay to give yourself some compassion.

Refuse the Excuses

If you know that the manipulator that you around always have excuses, stop allowing them. Don't make excuses for them and stop listening to theirs. Three is always something with people that like to manipulate. They blame it on work, their upbringing, their mood, and just about everything else, like that forgives what they are doing or that it makes things okay. No, your manipulator does not deserve forgiveness just because he grew up in a home that thought manipulation was okay. You don't have to extend that compassion, nor should you.

Excuses are just ways of getting you to feel bad and allow the other party to do what they want. However, there is a serious problem with this; giving in to their pity party is just giving in to more manipulation. The only purpose that they had in telling you what was going on with them in the first place was to convince you that they deserved that right to manipulate or influence you in the first place. Don't allow them to excuse their behaviors like this, or you will end up regretting it.

Maintain Good Relationships

Maintaining good relationships with other people out of the home is a great way for you to make sure that you can avoid being manipulated. Solid relationships with other people are one of the biggest ways that people end up off of the manipulator's list in the first place. The more people that are close to you, the more threats the manipulator has to deal with. Every single person that you are close to effectively acts as another boundary between you and being under the manipulator's utter control in the first place. Of course, he doesn't want to deal with that—he wants to be able to take complete control of the situation to ensure that ultimately, he can get what he wants.

Make sure that you recognize that any attempts to isolate you are probably ill-intentioned. Remember that when someone tries to control you, they want you as vulnerable as possible, and cutting you off from other people is one of the greatest ways to make that happen.

If you can keep those relationships with other people, you defend yourself. Likewise, if you have several friends voicing their concerns about someone, you would be well advised to consider what they are saying. Are they trying to protect you? Is the person a problem? He may very well be—and you need to face that fact. Think about what they say and give it the consideration that they deserve. Most of the time, your good friends that have healthy relationships with you won't feel threatened by you making friends with other people, and they won't voice that they have a problem lightly or without having a good reason to do so.

Work on Self-Esteem

Finally, one of the best things that you can do is make sure that you have a good, solid shield against being manipulated or abused is making sure that you protect your self-esteem. Make sure that you are always working to keep yourself safe by ensuring that you recognize that there is no reason for you to give in to the manipulation in the first place. By making sure that you have solid self-esteem, reminding yourself that you can, and you should, rely only on yourself and your abilities, you can ensure that you can resist.

So many of the manipulative tactics that you have seen in this book have involved giving in to feelings of inadequacy, guilt, or wanting to be involved with people somehow. If you can remind yourself that you don't have to validate yourself with other people's judgment of you, you can usually find that you are much happier and, therefore, more resilient to the manipulation tactics and common attempts to abuse you.

Get Therapy

Finally, consider getting therapy to help yourself to defend against manipulation. Especially if you have been on the receiving end before, there is a good chance that several of your very good, beneficial personality traits are being taken advantage of, and that is a problem. However, you can learn how you can overcome that. You can learn to figure out what it will take for you to better yourself over time. You can learn everything that you will need to know about making sure that you are happier, that you are less of a target, and in doing so, you can learn how to resist future attempts at manipulation. There is nothing wrong with getting therapy, and while it has had a stigma in the past, the truth is, it is something that just about every person could benefit from in some way.

Conclusion

Thank you for making it through to the end of *Dark Psychology The Secrets Revealed.* Hopefully, as you read through this book, you felt informed, enlightened, and empowered over everything that you would need to know to understand dark psychology to better protect yourself against it. Dark psychology can be terrifying, and manipulators are everywhere, but you can learn to protect yourself against them.

At this point, you've learned about several different types of manipulation and dark psychologies that exist. You've gotten to see into the mind of a narcissist. You've learned about several common forms of manipulation that are both compelling and effective. The tactics that are found in this book are some of the more common attempts to control you that you are likely to encounter. Many of the tidbits of advice that you received about fighting off manipulation should be effective in helping you to remain strong and able to resist the manipulation that you may eventually face.

From here, all that's left for you to do is take some time to begin learning what you can do to help yourself both use these tools for your good and make sure that you take the time to protect not just yourself, but also everyone around you. Make sure that you use the information that you got to work with those that you care about and to protect the unsuspecting. Ultimately, the tools that you have been provided in this book can be used for either good or bad purposes. You can choose to hurt or help. However, you have to be willing to deal with the consequences of what you decide to do.

Thank you once more for taking the time to read through this book. Hopefully, as you did, you found that there was plenty of great information. As you read through this book, you should have begun to feel more confident than you have been before. You should be ready to get out there and get started with your newfound information that you have gained. Don't let yourself be taken advantage of and learn that you, too, can fight back, protect yourself, and ensure that you can maintain yourself and your integrity.

And before we wrap up for good, please consider heading over to Amazon to leave a quick review with what you thought of the book! No matter whether you are new to understanding manipulation or you have been victimized in the past, hopefully, you feel a bit more confident and in control! Good luck with your future endeavors and growth that you will need to ensure your happiness!

Stoicism
And the Art Of Happiness

A Perfectly Balanced Match for Boosting Mental Toughness, Analyzing People, and Strengthening Emotional Intelligence. A Beginner's Guide to the Empathic and Stoic Way of Life

Daniel Brown

force on the date of publishing and subsequent time thereafter. All additional works derived from this material may be claimed by the holder of this copyright.

The data, depictions, events, descriptions, and all other information forthwith are considered to be true, fair, and accurate unless the work is expressly described as a work of fiction. Regardless of the nature of this work, the Publisher is exempt from any responsibility of actions taken by the reader in conjunction with this work. The Publisher acknowledges that the reader acts of their own accord and releases the author and Publisher of any responsibility for the observance of tips, advice, counsel, strategies, and techniques that may be offered in this volume.

Table of Contents

Introduction

Stop and think about the word stoicism for a moment—most people immediately conjure up the image of someone standing, blank faced and unmoving, physically and emotionally. It is easy to get caught up in the word's meaning, which, according to the dictionary, is:

Stoic: A person who can endure pain or hardship without showing their feelings or complaining.

All too often, however, people misunderstand that definition. Instead of not showing feelings or complaints, many people instead jump to the conclusion that if there are no emotions on the surface, then there are probably no emotions under the surface either. They assume that to be stoic, you must be cruel, or at the very least, emotionally shut off and blank. What they are missing, however, is that you can be outwardly blank, hiding the pains or struggles that you are suffering through, while internally still having all sorts of emotions. Just because you do not show your emotions outwardly does not mean that they are not there—it just means that you are in control of them.

Likewise, people tend to misunderstand what it means to be empathic. They assume that the empath is some emotionally volatile wreck who cannot walk into a crowded room without melting down at all of the emotions around them that they are sensing. This, too, is a bit of a misconception. You can be empathic, but also in control of your emotions as well. Both empaths and stoics share one thing in common: You are working to better yourself. Contrary to popular belief, you can be stoic and empathic at the same time—there is no real dichotomy between the two. They can be one and the same without a problem— you just have to be willing to work to allow both to be present at the same time.

Within this book, we are going to be addressing both stoicism and becoming an empathic individual. You can do both if you know what you are doing and you are willing to put in the effort. As you read through this book, you will discover that you can not only tap into your ability to understand other people, but also to allow yourself to be unburdened of the control of your emotions.

Ultimately, emotions are very important, and they hold a special power over us—they control us and influence what it is that we do and how we interact with the world. They are there to instinctively guide you through life so that you can stay alive. We evolved them for a reason—and that reason was for instincts.

As you read through this book, you will first be introduced to the idea of the empath, and from there, you will start to understand the stoic as well. The idea that you will be working toward is that it is possible to live a life that will embrace both concepts, recognizing that there is, in fact, a way to balance out stoicism with empathic life values to discover the perfect way to approach the world. If you can do that, you will find that you will be able to enjoy life much more. You will be able to reject the idea of dichotomies; you can be stoically empathic, or empathically stoic, and you will actually see that being able to innately and deeply understand humankind around you while also being able to restrain yourself from being controlled by those feelings is actually a highly beneficial way to get through life. If you can balance out stoicism with empathy, you get the best of both worlds all at once—you are able to live virtuously.

Chapter 1: Stoicism Vs. the Empath

To begin, we have to stop and look at both the empath and the stoic. Upon understanding both of them, we can begin to paint a picture of the stoic empath, someone who is able to feel deeply without becoming frenzied or passionate. It is someone who is able to retain control over themselves, even when things seem bleak or frustrating. As we read through this chapter, we will be going over the basic understanding of what the principles of stoicism are, what the idea behind an empath is, and what happens when you combine the two together.

The Purpose of Emotions and Empathy

Emotions and empathy are important—so important that we have them deeply ingrained into us. We have specifically evolved to have both emotions and empathy, as evidenced in the brain. We have areas in the brain that are specific to various emotions, and structures within the brain that are specific to regulating them. The amygdala, for example, a small structure deep in the brain, is responsible for the integration of emotions, behavior, and motivation. Empathy is equally important to the evolution of humanity—we are naturally empathetic to the point that we have mirror neurons—neurons throughout the brain that activate when you see someone else doing something.

For example, if you see someone else laughing, the area in your brain that controls laughter activates—but only the mirror neurons. You can understand the emotions and actions of others through these empathetic motor neurons—but why do we have them? Are they really as important as they seem?

Defining emotions

Emotions, then, are the feelings that we have—they are motivators. Emotions have three distinct parts to them:

- **The subjective component:** This is how you experience the emotion that you are having

- **The physiological component:** This is the response that your body has to the emotion that you are having

- **The expressive component:** This is the behavioral response that you have to your emotions

Each of these elements plays a part in the idea of an emotion, motivating us into action. They are there specifically for that point. Think about the last time you watched an animal walking around—they clearly feel emotions to some degree. Dogs, for example, can very clearly feel happiness, sadness, guilt, anger, and fear without a problem. We know this. We can tell when they are happy and sad. They have these emotions because they drive behaviors that are evolutionarily valuable. We feel fear to avoid something to keep ourselves alive. We get angry to protect ourselves from a perceived threat. We are happy to reinforce a behavior again. We are simple creatures at heart—our emotions are there to guide us if we let them.

However, emotions are not all-powerful. Notice how they are listed as motivational, but not as controlling. Emotions cannot control you unless you surrender yourself to them, known as letting yourself be led by passions. Passions, according to stoicism, should not be able to control you. We will be going over these in depth later in the book.

Emotions are only as powerful as you allow them to be—if you allow them to lead your behavior, they will. However, you can also learn to overcome them completely; you can discover what you can do to prevent yourself from being led by them. This is the entire premise behind stoicism—you do not let yourself be ruled by emotions.

The seven universal emotions

Most people think of emotions as wide reaching—we have joy and delight and excitement, but in reality, they are all subsets of just seven universal emotions.

These emotions are universal because we can identify them in all cultures around the world—even people born blind who have never actually seen a human face before still exhibit these emotions accurately and with the right facial expressions, leading to the belief that these emotions are innate rather than created through learning.

The seven emotions that are deemed universal in humans include:

- **Happiness:** This is the rewarding emotion that you feel when you do something good or right. It is meant to encourage you to repeat those behaviors in the future.

- **Sadness:** Sadness occurs when you do something wrong. It is the emotion that comes along with intense suffering, in which something was lost. It is meant to reinforce that a behavior should not be repeated.

- **Anger:** Anger is necessary to protect yourself—it is there so that you will be able to prevent yourself from any problems with violence. When you are threatened, you will get angry so that you can protect yourself.

- **Fear:** Fear is meant to influence you to run away from a situation to protect yourself. It is the precursor to anger and directly related to the fight or flight response in people. Fear is considered flight, while anger is considered the fight response.

- **Disgust:** Disgust is meant to keep you from consuming something that is toxic or unhealthy for you. When you feel disgusted, your body feels like it is repulsed by something—it wants to get away. This is meant to prevent you from eating, for example, rotten meat.

- **Surprise:** This is meant to redirect your attention and make you focus. When you feel surprised, you stop and look at what is happening around you and identify whatever it was that was not quite right and caught you by surprise.

- **Contempt:** Contempt is sort of like anger meets disgust—it is meant to be an emotion that makes you want nothing to do with someone. Effectively, it makes you look down on someone, unwilling to spend time with that individual any longer.

Defining empathy

With emotions out of the way, let's take a look at empathy. This is one of the defining features of the empath—they are highly empathetic, but what does that mean? Empathy is commonly accepted as the ability of someone to sense the emotions of someone else, as well as being able to understand, to some degree, what the other person is most likely feeling or thinking. It can be physical or emotional. It can involve understanding the position that someone else is in, or it can involve being able to feel their emotions yourself. There are all sorts of ways in which empathy plays out, and they all vary greatly from each other.

Empathy is incredibly important—it teaches us how to cooperate with each other. It helps us to create friendships or to make decisions that are moral and fair. It helps us help other people who are in need, and we can start to see signs of empathy in even young children and infants. It is there for a very good reason. In particular, it is believed that empathy may have evolved for a very specific reason—in particular, it is there to help to facilitate communication between people. It behaves as a sort of social signal to other people—you can communicate nonverbally when everyone is on the same page.

Think about it—if you are out walking and you see someone threatening behind a tree, but your friends in the group that are just a bit behind you cannot see them, what is the appropriate thing to do? You will probably freeze up at the sight of someone else as your body processes what to do next—and your friends that are behind you, being empathetic, can pick up on the fact that you are afraid, and it puts them on high alert. Now, they are aware that there is a problem instead of walking in blindly to a situation that could be potentially dangerous.

Humans are a social species, and because of that, we need to consider that nonverbal communication is highly important. This is why we have so many physical cues in general—human body language is highly complex. We are able to communicate nonverbally in all sorts of manners, and empathy tends to help with that. It also aids in bonding as well as cooperative behavior so that, as social animals, we are able to communicate even if we cannot use words.

The types of empathy

Empathy comes in all sorts of forms as well, but it is typically broken down into just three different types:

- **Cognitive empathy:** This is being able to know how someone else is feeling and what they may be thinking about at that moment. It is often also referred to as perspective taking. It is thinking and understanding what is going on. Think of this as if you stopped to negotiate something for work. If you notice that the other person's body language is closed off, you will get that sense that they are not feeling very open through cognitive empathy. You will think, "Wow! That person is not very open at all. What can I do to fix this problem?"

- **Emotional empathy:** This form of empathy is a bit different—it concerns itself with the feelings and sensations of someone else. This is where those mirror neurons come into play. When you look at someone else, you will then physically feel the other person's emotions as your own. Your own mirror neurons activate, and you suddenly feel those same feelings.

- **Compassionate empathy:** Finally, we take a look at compassionate empathy. This is the idea that you are able to feel the emotions that someone else is feeling while still being able to cognitively understand what they are thinking as well. It takes both the cognitive and compassionate sides and puts them together to create action.

Rationality Vs. Emotionality

You have all sorts of emotions for varying reasons. However, one thing is certain—your thoughts influence your emotions, and your emotions influence your behaviors. When you consider this endless cycle of thoughts, emotions, and behaviors, you realize that you have a method of controlling them built into this cycle. With thoughts, you can tame your emotions.

We typically can behave either rationally or emotionally at any point in time. Typically, you cannot rationally behave emotionally—they are like two ends of a spectrum. However, you can learn to recognize both the importance of logic and rationality while still being an emotional person. It is well within your power to be able to feel those emotions and let them act as informants about your current situation.

Your body feels those emotions for a reason, after all, and if you can identify why you feel those ways, you can use those interpretations to respond logically and responsibly. You could, for example, tell yourself that you are feeling scared because you realize that you are walking in an area in which you got into a car accident a year prior. When you identify the reason for those emotions, the emotions lose power to the rationality.

This is where stoicism and empathy will come into play together—you can use them at the same time, allowing for your empathy to let those emotions play their roles while still making sure that you are able to rationalize what is happening at the same time. You can think about the emotions. You can identify why you have those emotions. When you do that, you realize that you have more skills and capabilities than you ever realized. You can defeat that need to behave emotionally. You can remove the need for you to feel like you are a slave to your passions, something that we will be discussing very deeply later in this book as we tackle stoicism.

Introducing the Empath

Elysia is a 20-years-old college student studying social work. She is highly empathetic—she has not once seen a movie where someone died without tearing up or sometimes even crying. She feels sad when her friends around her are sad, and she also picks up on tension as soon as she walks through the door. Of course, that worked both ways—sometimes, she would be surrounded by positive, happy people and couldn't feel better. She loved it when she was able to enjoy other people around her or when the energy in a room was just right. Elysia never figured out quite how to explain the way that she felt... Until the day that she stumbled upon the word *empath* online.

Highly sensitive. Attuned to the emotions of others. Struggles with personal boundaries. The more that she read the traits of the empath, the more it made sense—she was also a highly sensitive empath.

Elysia struggled with her boundaries. She would often let people walk all over her because she would rather sacrifice herself than make someone else unhappy. She regularly allowed other people to rule over her. She allowed all sorts of transgressions to slide because she feared rocking the boat too much or making other people miserable. As an empath, she had some serious work to do if she wanted to be able to get through life without letting every negative emotion, she passed wash over her.

Empaths are often defined as too sensitive or emotional. They are typically identified by being told that they need to calm down or stop reacting so much. However, that is not entirely fair to accuse them of. Empaths themselves are people who are highly sensitive—in particular, they are highly sensitive to the emotions and potentially even the thoughts of those around them. They are usually able to pick up on signs that most people do not realize, and because they are able to do so, they also unintentionally tend to make themselves suffer as well.

They often take on the emotions of the people around them as well, which is where that reputation comes in. When a highly sensitive person is in a room full of bad energy or vibes, they usually feel miserable. They feel stressed out or annoyed with the interactions that they are getting, and because of that, they start to struggle with their emotions. For the empath, it is difficult to define where their emotions begin and where they end. However, it is highly possible to understand those differences over time. It is quite simple to be able to define where those feelings start and end if you learn how to do so, and that is a critical skill for all empaths to know.

Introducing Stoicism

John is a quiet 27-years old man. He tries to remind himself that keeping himself rooted firmly in the realm of logic is the best way to control himself. We are, after all, cognitively rational creatures. We are designed to have this ability—but we have to make sure that we make it a point to tap into it, after all. He spends his time working diligently without complaint. Even when he is asked to stay late, he is willing to put in that effort. Even when he doesn't want to, he is happy to do so because he knows that it is for the best.

Most of John's friends would describe him as cold or unfeeling, but that could not be further from the truth—he is quite emotional, but he makes sure that is mind is in control at all times. He understands that we have emotions and that they have a purpose, but more than anything else, he also recognizes that he is able to influence and control those emotions so that he is able to control himself as well.

As a Stoic, he was content, knowing that he would be able to control himself. He did know that emotions mattered to him, but usually, he wanted to focus on thinking rationally. After all, we have those passions, and they usually get us into trouble.

Stoicism, and the followers, known as Stoics, are highly rational individuals. They focus on the idea that logic matters more than everything else. Derived from the Greek philosopher, Zeno of Citium, Stoicism focuses on the nature of the soul, learning about the nature of the mind and referring to it as having an internal heat or fire, known as the pneuma, or the soul. The pneuma was identified as being various actions that were performed by the individuals; it was the world-soul; it worked to motivate and drive us.

Stoics, then, attempted to control that pneuma to achieve Eudaimonia—utter happiness or blessedness. Eudaimonia is believed to be achieved through controlling and accepting the moment. This means that, for the Stoic, being able to control oneself is the utmost pleasure. It is to recognize the virtue within humans—the good deeds that we do. It rejects the idea that you must have external material belongings to be happy.

To the Stoics, they recognize the world as being an amalgamation of logic, physics, and naturalistic ethics, focusing on human knowledge and what we have control over. It focuses on developing the self through being able to teach and fortify oneself against those destructive emotions that will otherwise cause problems, and through this path, it is possible to overcome everything.

Who Is the Stoic Empath?

When you look at the two, it is easy to see why so many people may believe in that false dichotomy—you see that the empaths are highly emotional, but at the same time, the Stoics are highly focused on controlling those negative emotions. Where, then, is the line drawn, you may ask?

Notice how the Stoics control their emotions and reactions while the empath feels them deeply. There is nothing about the two that are inherently delegitimizing of the other. It is entirely possible to follow the Stoic way of life while still being an empath, and doing so is actually a great way to achieve power.

In fact, Stoicism actually promotes the use of empathy and being empathetic toward other people. It is highly important to the Stoics that people should pay close attention to others, listening to them, and acknowledging that what they say is valid.

Marcus Aurelius, one of the most famous Stoics, wrote that we must be able to pay close attention to what other people are saying, making sure that we are able to, as he put it, "enter[ing], so far as possible, into the mind of the speaker," in his famous *Meditations,* Book 6, line 53. Is that not highly indicative of empathy right there? That is effectively the definition of cognitive empathy, and here is Marcus Aurelius, encouraging it.

It is emphasized even more later as well in his *Meditations*—he also discusses, in book 7, line 4, that "In conversation, one should attend closely to what is being said, and with regard to every impulse attend to what arises from it; in the latter case, to see from the first what end it has in view, and in the former, to keep a careful watch on what people mean to say."

He is effectively encouraging the followers of Stoicism to not only pay attention to the words that are being said but also paying close attention to the way that it is said. It advocates for paying attention to the impulse—the emotions—behind the actions and the words. He is pushing the point that we should all be looking at each other empathetically, even in stoicism, for when we can identify the way that other people are feeling, we can then begin to see the truth of what was meant to be said. We are able to understand deeper, to be able to comprehend the truest intentions of the words being said.

The Stoic empath, then, is someone who does this—it is someone who is following the truths of Stoicism, following those principles and making sure to live the life working toward virtue, while still recognizing that emotions are important. They can see exactly what value comes from emotions and being able to use them, and they tend to encourage the usage of those emotions so that they can get the most out of the situation.

Chapter 2: Understanding the Empath

Empathy is to make ourselves vulnerable and open—
it is to welcome in the emotions of others, no matter
what they are. Sometimes, this can be highly
inconvenient; when it happens, you can
unintentionally find yourself in a bad spot in which
you are stuck with someone else's bad emotions, and
that can be difficult to deal with. Empathy, however,
is also highly powerful. It is healing. It helps us to
reach out to others, to connect, and to be able to really
understand the situations of others, to develop that
compassion and desire to help. Some of the most
kindhearted people in the world are empaths, highly
driven by their desire to help other people because
they can feel those emotions emanating off of people,
and it hurts.

They see someone who is hungry on the side of the
road with a sign, and they want to cry. They want to
be able to relate better. They want to connect, even
when it feels like it is too much. However, the empaths
sometimes get burnt out after a while; after enough

time, they start to feel like they are too emotional, or they cannot cope with the negative or foreign emotions that they are filled with.

As we read through this chapter, we are going to be taking a look at some of the most common traits of the empath to get a better understanding of who they are, what they do, and how they behave. If you can understand this as an empath, you can start to see some of the traits that you may never have even realized that you possess. These traits and emotions are highly influential and can even be overwhelming ad annoying sometimes, but they are important to recognize so that you do understand the ways that you engage with the world around you.

The more that you begin to understand how you navigate through the world, the sooner that you can start to fix the actions that are not beneficial to you— and stoicism later can actually help you greatly with doing so.

Now, let's take a look at nine of the most major traits of empaths in general. Keep in mind that these are generalizations of the empath specifically—they are not specific to empathy itself, but rather to the highly sensitive empath.

Empaths Absorb Emotions

Empaths, by definition, are highly empathetic to *something*. Most of them are particularly in tune with the emotions of other people—they find themselves driven specifically by the feelings that other people have at any point in time and take on the emotions of others. This is believed to be caused by overactive mirror neurons—the neurons that are responsible for the empathizing in people who are not highly empathetic.

Imagine this for a moment—if you walk into a room, does your mood suddenly shift? Do you often find yourself furious when someone else is, or deeply moved when you hear someone else struggling and crying? If you find that your mood usually reflects people around you, there is a good chance that you are empathic, and that can bring with it its own handful of struggles if you are not careful. You will need to make sure that, when you do interact with people, you pay special attention to the emotions of other people, and you must always make sure that you ask yourself if you are feeling the emotions of someone else or if you are feeling your own.

Think of emotions, for empaths, as highly contagious—the emotional contagion highly impacts them and renders them entirely caught up in what they are doing. They get stuck with the emotions of the people around them, and they cannot do anything about it. However, they can learn to differentiate themselves from those emotions so that they can do better.

Empaths Struggle in Public

Because empaths tend to absorb the emotions of other people, they typically struggle greatly when it comes to getting out in public. The public can be highly overwhelming for them, and they can feel like they are stuck. They can feel overwhelmed by the constant inundation of emotions from strangers walking by. Because they are highly empathetic to people, they pick up those feelings as they go by.

When this happens, they can feel like they are getting emotional whiplash; it is possible that the emotions are constantly swirling around, draining the empath until they can no longer tolerate being out in those crowds, and they need to retreat. This typically garners empaths with the designation of introverted—people who find that being around other people is highly draining.

Think of it like going into public is like running a marathon. You must constantly be fending off all of those negative feelings as you go through your day, and that can be entirely overwhelming. It can be difficult at times to even tell if the mood that you are feeling is your own or someone else's, and because of that, it can be tough to figure out how to react and how to treat those around you. You may end up with a reputation of being too reactive or too unstable when, in reality, you were just responding to the world around you.

Empaths Feel the Energy in the Room

If you are not an empath, you may not quite understand this one, but any empath will know immediately what is meant by this. When you walk into a room as an empath, you will feel the energy in the room immediately. You cannot help it—all around you; you feel the constant energy from people. You do not need to talk to anyone to tell the mood when you first enter the room in the first place. When you enter, you simply begin to pick up on the cues enough to understand what you will need to know if you want to mesh with the group.

The empaths will almost always read the mood of a room just right. They pick it up on their own, subconsciously picking up all of the body language in the room and taking it on as their own. As their mirror neurons activate when they enter the room, they pick up on tensions if they are high. They can see when people are having a good time or struggling to have a difficult conversation, even if there is nothing readily apparent externally that will betray what is being discussed.

Empaths Understand the Perspectives of Others

Because of the skills that empaths have when it comes to reading the feelings of others, they are also able to pick up on perspectives readily and easily. This is a great benefit, but also a major struggle at the same time. As an empath, you will be able to tell why people are doing what they are doing. You never judge people for their actions—rather, you take time to understand the background information as well.

Think of a situation in which you may have seen someone do something that was, objectively speaking, wrong. Maybe they stole a loaf of bread or a gallon of milk from the grocery store, but they were caught as they tried to leave. When you hear the man sobbing about how hungry his toddler is, you can't help but feel bad for him. Did he do a bad thing? Absolutely—stealing is, objectively speaking, and legally speaking, verboten.

You know that it is not allowed, but still, you do not feel like the person is a bad one. You know that his heart was in the right place—he wasn't out there stealing lobster and cigarettes or alcohol—he was stealing basic supplies for his young, hungry child ad you could not find any real way to fault him for that, even though you knew it was wrong.

Taking the perspective of other people can be a great asset, but it can also come back to cause problems if you are not careful.

Empaths Attract People in Need of Help

More often than not, empaths have a way of attracting people who are in need of help. They are simply approachable, and while they may not like to admit it or to deal with it in the moment, they are usually happy to help—helping is in their nature, and they struggle to turn away someone in need of assistance for any reason.

Whether for advice that is needed, such as about a difficult topic or something about how to react to someone else, or even just needing directions, something about empaths is warm and inviting to those needing something. Empaths, despite typically being quite reserved, find themselves constantly approached for all sorts of reasons, to the point where they assume that it is normal to be approached—until their friends mention that it is strange how often they are approached on the regular.

Empaths are also typically highly supportive of people, and that can attract even more people to them. They are usually willing and ready to listen, even if it is something difficult for them to deal with. Of course, that usually then leads to drained energy reserves and feeling burnt out at the end of the day as well. However, the empath will do it anyway to help those in need.

Empaths Struggle with Difficult News

When empaths are exposed to difficult news, they tend to struggle. They may see that someone was in a horrible accident and start to cry for them—even though they have no true idea who the individual was.

They may never have even heard of that individual, but they still struggled to cope with the news. For empaths, hearing about people suffering, no matter what happened to lead up to it, is too much.

Empaths may get upset at hearing about violence, and when it comes to hearing bad news from one of their friends and family members, they struggle to cope with it. They find that it is just too much to bear, and it can be incredibly draining for them. Oftentimes, the negative news can cause them to feel strong emotions even when really, there is no direct impact on them. This sensitivity has its pace, but it can also be difficult to deal with.

Any sort of tragedy is painful, real, or fictional. Any sort of television shows, even where it is clearly fiction, is enough to bring on the waterworks. It can be difficult to watch sometimes, and empaths sometimes even go out of their ways to avoid the content if they can when they find it to be too emotionally triggering. They would rather simply remain out of the loop than continue to suffer with it.

Empaths Love Pets and Babies

While empaths typically struggle with adults and the emotions that they bring, they typically find solace in the company of both babies and pets. There is just something about the pure, unbridled joy of both pets and babies that can be quite recharging and even relaxing and bring them the peace that they may need after a long, hard day of dealing with the emotions of other people.

Empaths Struggle with Emotional Contagion

For empaths, emotional contagion is very real. You can see this oftentimes in even babies—it has been found that if one newborn in a hospital ward starts to cry, the whole ward may start to cry in return. One person talking about their anxiety can also start everyone else to feel anxiety as well. However, for the empaths, it is worse—it is more intense and difficult to cope with. They struggle to deal with the negativity that they sometimes get from other people. They know that it is not good for them, but they often struggle to really identify in the moment whether the emotions belong to them or to someone else.

The emotions that the empath feels are real, even if they are not theirs in origin. They still feel the same strong emotions going through them. They still have the same physical reaction that other people have, but they simply did not share the same cause. However, that does not mean that you can just tell an empath to get over it and move on, or to stop overreacting. Rather, you have to support them and make sure that they understand that it is valid to feel such strong emotions no matter what.

Empaths Struggle in Relationships

Another common trait of the empath is struggling in relationships. For empaths, they find that it is difficult to keep themselves separate from their partners—they struggle to maintain those fine boundaries between themselves and other people. As those boundaries blur, it gets harder to make sure that you are maintaining your own privacy or your own personality. For many empaths, it can be easy to get caught up in the idea that you have to take on the same likes, opinions, and general thoughts as the other people.

This is exacerbated by the fact that you may spend longer periods of time with your partner, especially if you live together. It is natural for you, as an empath, to start to get caught up in their emotions and thoughts without thinking about it. However, it is highly important that you are able to make sure that you keep your own autonomy. Boundaries have to be maintained, and when they start to fall, there are very real problems.

Empaths Are Easy Targets for Abuse

Because of the fact that empaths are so emotionally available for everyone around them and they naturally try to see the best in everyone, trying to take on the perspectives of other people rather than taking a look at a situation based on black and white views of a situation, they are very easy to take advantage of. People who are highly empathetic usually try to listen to all of the potential excuses that are supposed to be there to justify the abuse that they are experiencing. They may tell themselves that it is not the fault of the abuser that they are repeating behaviors that they learned growing up, or they may tell themselves that really, the abuse was their fault, not the fault of the abuser.

They are so empathetic and so desperate to see the good in other people that they tend to forget that ultimately, they are not responsible for everyone around them. There are no rules that say that they must be responsible for every little thing that happens to them—in fact, it is the opposite. They must learn to recognize that they are at risk of becoming codependent if they are not careful.

Empaths Need Time Alone

Finally, a very common trait of an empath is the need for alone time—they need to spend time away from other people so that they can relax and recharge. The alone time is crucial, and they may even say that they need to be left alone from their partners as well, sometimes. This is not because they dislike the people around them—they just need a respite from feeling everyone else's feelings as well. It can be highly overwhelming to constantly feel what everyone else is feeling around them. If you are an empath, make sure that you get that time for yourself. If you know an empath, always respect when they ask for that privacy.

Chapter 3: Pros and Cons of the Empath's Power

Now, it may seem like being an empath is more of a problem than a blessing, and in many ways, it can be. However, the empathic abilities of someone else are not a curse—they are a blessing, and they need to be treated in that manner. It may take you some time to get to know those feelings and abilities for what they really are, but if you can get used to the way that you think or adjust yourself to the interactions that you have with other people, you will find that being empathetic can actually be both one of your greatest assets and worst weaknesses that you have.

It is very important for you to understand what it means to be and live as an empath. It is hard to identify the empath sometimes, but when they are identified, usually, you can figure out that they actually have some pretty wonderful abilities that they may not usually advertise or broadcast widely. Yes, being empathic can have some cons—but so can anything else. It is normal for something to have pros and cons, and it is next to impossible to ever have something that is completely free of any negative aspects. We are not perfect beings—we all have our pros and cons. We all have our strengths and weaknesses, but it is when you learn to identify them and use them that you will be able to really begin to understand yourself.

Pros to Being an Empath

Being an empath is not all bad—not by a long shot. There are many different skills and traits related to being an empath that can actually be quite beneficial if you can learn to harness them. Your abilities are a gift, and these are the ways that you can count on your powers to benefit you at some point in your life.

You are strongly in tune with the emotions of others

When you are able to pay attention to how other people feel, and you are able to pick up on those emotions without having to try, you can take advantage of that fact. There are many different situations in which you will be able to make use of reading the emotions of other people—it is highly beneficial if, for example, you have to work with people. Imagine that you are a salesperson for a moment. If you can read other people with ease, you can start to make use of that. You can change your own behaviors to try to influence other people. We are naturally social beings, after all, and we tend to interact closely with each other.

If you notice that someone is nervous about closing the deal, for example, you can be more reassuring, offering all of the necessary evidence to show them that they do not have to worry so much. If the other person is too closed off to get very far in negotiations, you can work to open them up to make sure that they actually want to be willing to close the deal. You will be able to make use of your skills to help other people in these ways.

Alternatively, you will also be able to pick up on dangerous situations. If the feelings that you pick up on are bad enough, you can usually figure out why and you will then be able to react accordingly. If someone is giving you bad vibes, there is probably a reason for it. Trust your gut, empath—it is almost always right.

You love and feel compassion deeper than the average person

Your emotions are also quite magnified when you are empathic. This is not because of anything that you do—rather, you simply tend to love and feel compassion more than other people. This is something that is difficult for empaths to deal with, but it should be accepted as genuine. In fact, the amount of love and compassion that you feel can even be almost overwhelming sometimes.

As an empath, the feelings that you have are intense, and they will be further magnified when you catch onto the feelings of your partner as well. It can be difficult for the empath to navigate relationships with others just due to the sheer extreme level of interaction that you have in relationships and just how overwhelming they can become, but when you are able to embrace and harness that propensity for love and compassion, you can get far in life.

That compassion can also be channeled toward work as well—many empaths naturally find themselves wanting to find a job in which they are able to help other people as much as possible. They are driven to become the teachers for tomorrow's generation. They want to become social workers to help other people escape abusive situations or break free from poverty's grasp. They want to make sure that they are able to do the most good in the world as possible—even if that comes with the territory of being surrounded by people that are too difficult to be around, or being around hard emotions to handle.

You are a fantastic judge of character

When you first meet someone or even get into a situation that stirs strong emotions in you, you learn pretty quickly to trust those gut reactions. You are fantastic at judging the character of people just because of the fact that you are so in tune with everyone around you. You may catch onto things that you cannot understand why you know them. You may realize that you are asking questions that are related to a specific trauma. You may ask them if they are struggling with something that is entirely related to what you are talking about—because you have a hunch, and you have to find out if you are right.

Likewise, you are likely to find that your strong negative impulses or assumptions are right as well. If you feel that someone is going to be a bad idea to hang around, you should probably trust that gut instinct—it is there for a reason, and it is not going to steer you wrong. Empaths can sense the intentions of other people; they can tell when someone is approaching them with the intention to harm them or to be kind. This sort of internal radar can be incredibly useful for you when you are out and about. The intuition that you have is incredible and one of the greatest tools that you can have.

You can identify liars

You will be able to tell when someone is lying. It can be kind of hard to explain, but you may get a feeling in your gut that the other person is lying, whether they have indicated that they are lying or not. This is quite powerful—if you need to talk to people and get honesty for work, this is a great way to do so. If you want to make sure that you are not being lied to, you will be able to do that.

Of course, this has other implications as well—if you can tell when someone is lying to you, you are going to be able to protect yourself. If you can tell that someone else is trying to manipulate you, you can break free from that—you can tell yourself that you will not be tolerating that kind of behavior and refuse to engage with it. You will be able to follow that intuition, and if you do not, you will probably learn pretty quickly that you should have listened to it the first time.

Cons to Being an Empath

Of course, there are also all sorts of cons to being highly empathic as well, but those can be worked through with time. Make sure that you are acutely aware of the cons that you are likely to face—when you know what your weaknesses are, you will be able to guard against them and prevent these cons from actually controlling you. When you learn to protect yourself, these cons will not be nearly as bad as they would be if you left them entirely unguarded—learn to recognize the warning signs and respect them for what they are so that you can protect yourself, no matter what happens.

You feel the emotions of other people

Any empath would readily admit that the ability to feel the emotions of other people is both a blessing and a curse. It is great when you are able to use it, but sometimes, you can become overwhelmed. When you are constantly being impacted by the emotions of other people, you can find that it is difficult to concentrate. It can be draining, and even dangerous sometimes if you are constantly struggling with emotions.

You can even start to pick up strongly negative emotions as well—and those can leave you reeling and really struggling to interact well with people around you. If you are particularly sensitive, you may find that you are caught up in the anxiety or depression of other people, suffering from pain that is not yours, nor does it originate from you. Yes, you can use that information that you have to try to help yourself, but at the end of the day, you must remember that you have to protect yourself and your emotions. You need to be able to keep in mind that if your emotions are running high, you need to stop yourself and ask if they are yours or someone else's.

You are more likely to be overwhelmed

When you are highly sensitive, you are much more likely to get overwhelmed. This makes sense—you cannot push back at those negative emotions to protect yourself. They simply fester and eat at you until they are too much for you to bear. When you have no real way to stop those emotions, you find that you have to take other approaches instead, and that can be difficult sometimes when you are entirely unsure of how to change up your reactions.

Beyond just emotions, you are also likely to be highly susceptible to being overwhelmed by all sorts of other aspects of life as well. It could be that touch sets you off, or you could struggle with louder noises. Highly sensitive people can be sensitive to more than just emotions—senses can be overwhelming as well, and that sensitivity can make it so that you cannot properly cope with the struggles that you have at any point in time. It is also possible that your sensitivity can actually make you more susceptible to panic attacks and higher levels of anxiety as well, especially in situations in which you are struggling greatly with dealing with the emotions of other people.

You have mood swings

When you are empathic, you are likely to find that your emotions swing from end to end on the spectrum—you cannot help it; it happens on its own, and it can be incredibly detrimental to you and those around you. When you struggle to control your own mood because you are constantly reflecting the moods of other people, you can really struggle with yourself. You will be stuck, feeling entire as if you are a slave to those intense emotions if you are not careful. Your emotions will become your worst enemy as an empath if you cannot learn to manage them, and that is one of the hardest things for you to do.

Even worse, you will probably struggle to know which emotions are yours and which are those of other people. This means that, if you are inexperienced, you will probably find yourself wondering if you actually feel the way that you are feeling or if you are reflecting the feelings of other people—and it will oftentimes be kind of hard to tell the difference. However, you can learn to do exactly that if you work hard to protect yourself.

You may be more susceptible to using drugs or alcohol

Being empathic is draining for the best of us. It is utterly destructive for those who do not know what they are doing or for those who are unsure of how to approach the problem in the first place. All too often, people who are desperate for a respite from the constant inundation of emotion may find themselves instead shifting to drinking or using drugs in an attempt to escape the pain that comes along with the empathic nature of your mind.

Of course, unhealthy coping mechanisms are not going to help you at all—they are actually only going to make things worse. You need to make sure that you are able to make use of the right, healthier coping mechanisms that will help to take that edge off without having to resort to alcohol or drugs. You can learn to do it, and we will be going over some of these methods in the next chapter that you can use to protect yourself.

You are physically exhausted

As much as you are emotionally exhausted by your empathic abilities, you may be surprised to realize that you become physically drained as well—you may find that the emotions that you feel get so strong and overwhelming sometimes that you cannot help but feel that you are physically exhausted as well. This often happens in particular after becoming unable to cope with the sheer level of stimulation emotionally that you have received. The overstimulation drives you insane and makes it impossible for you to cope further. When this happens, you will need to find some other way for you to cope.

You may also have physical symptoms related to your physical exhaustion as well. Commonly, empaths will struggle with migraines or headaches, and may even suffer from their ears ringing as well. It is a sign that you have taken on too much and that you will need to recharge.

You are a common target for abuse

All sorts of people want to take advantage of you when you are highly empathic. This is because they can sense that you are the kind of person to whom they can give the benefit of the doubt, and therefore, it will be very easy to walk all over. When it comes right down to it, your empathic tendencies to be kind to everyone and to give everyone that you meet the benefit of the doubt can be quite harmful to you and works to essentially enable your abusers or those that are trying to manipulate you. You must learn to recognize that, even if you would never use someone else, other people are willing to be opportunistic and take any chance that they can get to take control of someone else for their own benefit.

Chapter 4: Protecting the Empathic Self

If you are an empath, you know the pain of being in a room that is just a bit too busy for you. You know the feeling of doubt, of your gut gnawing at itself because of what you are able to sense around you. You will be able to feel these intense feelings within you, stressing you out and putting you on edge. However, you do not have to feel these ways. You can learn to protect yourself so that you can avoid that constant discomfort.

Keep in mind that there is no such thing as a cure for the empath, nor is there any way for you to simply never be inconvenienced by the problem that you are having with absorbing the energy of others. However, recognize that you must make sure that you are able to protect yourself to lessen some of that drain. If you can lessen the drain, you can start to protect yourself from becoming overstimulated so that you can leave and find somewhere that you can recharge when the time is there.

As you read through these activities and methods that you can use to protect yourself from being completely overwhelmed by the energies around you, keep in mind that you will need to work well with yourself to protect yourself from suffering. Keep in mind that it will be a trial and error period while you figure out what works and what you prefer not to do. You need to figure out what will be the most beneficial to you and you alone and make sure that you always respect that need to escape when you need it. These methods will help to protect you, but you will still be susceptible to being drained.

Shielding Visualization

Shielding is a very popular method that empaths use to help them fortify themselves against the feelings of others that threaten to overwhelm them. When you are able to use shielding, you can effectively block out the toxic energy so that you are able to focus only on the positivity instead, protecting yourself and keeping up the energy that you want to absorb while rejecting the toxic stuff that is going to drain you faster than anything else.

This is a method that can be used anywhere, and you should do so any time that you feel like you need it. If you feel like you are in a bad spot suddenly, if you start to pick up on those bad vibes, it is time to summon that shield to protect yourself, and you can do this incredibly simple. All you have to do is become aware of the negative situation, trust yourself, and begin to visualize.

Take a few deep breaths, in and out, breathing slowly as you do. After a few deep breaths, imagine that there is a shield beginning to form around you. It could create a barrier in a great, big bubble around you, or it could be against your skin, protecting your body from the negative energy surrounding you. The shield should be protective and comforting. Visualize it to be beautiful and warm, and then imagine that it extends out just past you, at least a few inches away. As you do this, visualize the negative energy bouncing right off of it and away into the universe. As you do this, you will be able to keep yourself centered.

You will remind yourself that you are not feeling any negative emotions at that moment, and you will be able to reject them as not being yours. Likewise, you will be able to feel centered and energized as you do this. It will keep you safe and comfortable, even if you are somewhere that you would otherwise be stressed out by.

Expressing Your Needs

In relationships, it is very easy to get completely overwhelmed. It is difficult to put yourself first when you are an empath, and because of that, you may really struggle to help yourself figure out how to express what you want or what you need. You might struggle to assert those needs, even if you know that there will be no resistance over them if you were to mention them. You must make sure that you learn how you can express them with your partner so that you will be able to protect and care for yourself.

Keep in mind that, in a healthy relationship, your partner *wants* to know what it will take to keep you comfortable. Your partner *wants* you to be taken care of. Your partner does not want you to suffer. Because of this, you need to learn to find your voice. You need to learn to tell your partner what you need so that you do not suffer.

Start this by asking yourself what you need. What is it that you have been afraid to ask for? Do you need more time by yourself, or spent together? Do you need to find ways to engage with each other more? Be honest with each other and express those needs without any judgment. Let your partner know exactly how you feel. It will be harder at first, but over time, you can master this art and make sure that you are giving yourself and your partner the respect and relationship that you both deserve.

Setting Boundaries

Whether at home or at work, boundaries and empaths rarely mesh well, especially if the empath is not fully comfortable in his or her powers at that point in time. However, boundaries are essential. Like shielding, you can create a sort of barrier through which you block out the stress and protect your energy level. A common method to do this is to make use of a few small trinkets or items that have a deep meaning to you and then place them along the perimeter of the space that you are in.

For example, imagine that you are at work and your office tends to stress you out. Instead of giving into that stress, you decide that you are going to focus on blocking the stress out. You take a picture of your partner, or of your children, if applicable, and you place them on the edge of your desk. You can put objects that have a deep meaning as well—you could have, for example, a small stone that you keep on your desk or a religious object for the religion that you practice and place them at the edge of your desk. Plants are another common one that is used for the empath, creating a protective boundary that they can rely on to help them.

This effectively helps them to mute out any of the stress that is surrounding them. They are able to create an area in which they are willing to be entirely at ease at work or at home.

Preventing Overload

You must also be well aware of how you can prevent yourself from suffering from empathy overload. Empathy overload is that state at which you can no longer fight against the negativity that you are feeling—it is so overwhelming that it takes over, and you need to find some way to protect yourself.

However, if you can prevent yourself from getting to that overloaded state, you can prevent the meltdown that will otherwise come. If you are aware of the fact that you are absorbing stress, you can stop yourself from being able to release the negative energy. Some people will make use of essential oils, and others will make it a point to meditate or breathe deeply, imagining that as they breathe out, they are releasing their stressors and protecting themselves. No matter how you choose to do it, you are usually able to start feeling better quickly.

Make sure that in preventing overload, you need to balance the time that you spend with other people versus spending time with those around you. You want to make sure that the time that you spend with other people is highly effective, and this means that you need to also give yourself that recharge time on the regular. The only person that is going to protect you from burnout is yourself. This means that you must be mindful of your schedule and do not be afraid to reschedule if you have to.

Further, make sure that you make it a point to set clear boundaries with people that you know are toxic. You are allowed to say no to people, and even better, you owe nobody an explanation for why you are saying no in the first place. You do not have to justify why you will say no. Also, you must make sure that when you are trying to protect yourself from those meltdowns, you shield yourself effectively. Practice self-care and make sure that you are kind to yourself. Remind yourself that sometimes, the best that you can do is good enough, even if you did not get what you were trying to do done.

The Empathic Protector Meditation

When you need some extra guidance or another shield, a common meditation is to call upon a protector for yourself. Imagine this as being akin to your spirit animal or spiritual guide—it should be something that speaks to you spiritually, that makes you feel at ease. Some people like to use wolves or tigers. Others prefer smaller animals. Whatever it is, it should be something that can protect you and that you can envision fighting off the pain or negativity that is filling your heart. If you find that you are being overwhelmed rapidly with negativity before you are able to keep it out or protect yourself, try to make use of this meditation.

First, you must figure out what it is that you want to visualize. What kind of animal speaks to your heart? What do you feel an affinity for? Imagine that anima in the depths of your heart manifested of your very soul. When you are overwhelmed or teetering on the edge of becoming overwhelmed, stop, take a deep breath, and summon the image in your mind's eye.

As you summon that image of the great, big predator that is there to protect you, you can start to imagine it protecting you. Make sure that it carefully and thoroughly guards you; it should walk around you. It should make sure that none of that overwhelmingly negative energy gets through to you. It is patient. It is powerful. And, it can destroy and dissolve that negative energy for you.

Imagine that the protector is shielding you and protecting you. Imagine how it looks, how it looks to you, protecting you, and ensuring that you are not afraid. Imagine how it cares for you and how it looks to you like it can keep you safe. Feel the strength of the creature filling you and keeping you capable of continuing forward. Imagine that you are entirely protected.

This is something that you should be able to use at any moment. Save it for the last resort—whenever you are overwhelmed, or risking that point of being overwhelmed, use it. If you can keep it special and calming for you, you will be able to keep yourself steady no matter what you are facing.

Journal Regularly

As an empath, you probably fill up on negative energy on a regular basis, even if you do everything in your power not to. That energy has to be processed somehow, and a great way to do so is through the use of journaling. When you journal, you can protect yourself from those negative emotions. When you journal, you can release them out and begin to work through the thoughts that are circling around in your mind. You will be channeling the energy in your mind and heart to the paper, and in doing so, you get that power back over the situation.

Take the time every day to do this—spend time at night, preferably just before bed, releasing all of that pent up negativity so that you can be free of it for a restful sleep. When you do this, you are able to start relaxing over time. Being able to release that energy will help with your sleep and your mood, and you will be able to use it on a regular basis.

Avoid Toxic People

This should go without saying, but one of the greatest things that you can do for yourself as an empath is to make sure that you avoid anyone that is toxic. Make sure that, no matter what is happening, you make sure that you are paying close attention to the people around you. Make sure that you are avoiding the people in your life that are going to do nothing but harm you or bring you down. When you notice who the true toxic individuals are, from the narcissists to the abusers or anyone else that just wants to take advantage of you, you need to get away. You need to find ways that you can protect yourself, and for most people, that involves figuring out how to escape them and how you can stay away.

Remember this—no one is entitled to your time. No one is entitled to controlling or using you. No one is worth sacrificing everything for if all they want to do is take advantage of you. Respect yourself. Remember that you are valuable as well, and make sure that you protect yourself and your mind. If you feel like someone else seems dangerous, there is probably a reason for it. Do not let yourself fall for those traps of trying to justify it—negativity and toxicity are negative and toxic for a reason.

You wouldn't let a rattlesnake bite you just because it asked nicely, would you? So why let a toxic individual subject you to their negativity and potentially violence without a good reason to do so? Your only duty is to yourself, and you must do what it will take to protect yourself, even if that means cutting people off, regardless of who they are. There is no reason to let yourself be subjected to constant negativity, even if they are family.

Chapter 5: Finding Peace and Happiness as an Empath

The empath is sensitive—that cannot be avoided. However, just because you are sensitive and constantly inundated with a wide range of emotions does not mean that you cannot achieve utter happiness. You can learn to be at peace and happy with yourself—you just have to learn what it is that you need. You can learn to find both peace and happiness as an empath, protecting yourself from everything that you will likely experience if you were to not bother. If you know what you are doing, you can ensure that you are highly insulated against the stress and turmoil that emotional contagion can inflict upon you. You just have to learn to know what you are doing.

Within this chapter, we are going to look at what it is that the empath requires for happiness. These are the points and recommendations to remember if you want to be able to achieve and attain that happiness to ensure that ultimately, at the end of the day, you are able to cope with your larger than life feeling that you may sometimes suffer from. The sooner that you learn to overcome those emotions and protect yourself, the sooner that you can begin working to ensure that your thoughts and feelings are valid and able to protect you. All you need to do is follow these steps to achieve that inner peace.

Spend Time Alone

When you spend time alone as the empathic individual that you are, you are able to remind yourself that ultimately, you can recover. As someone that is highly reactive, you will want to make sure that you have the time where you are able to get away from everyone around you. It lets you stop and think about yourself and your reactions. It is easy to feel so caught up in the world around us that we cannot identify our own feelings. It is imperative that you are able to figure out exactly what you need to be happy so that you can, in fact, achieve it regularly, and oftentimes, that comes with the time alone to reflect quietly.

It is difficult to attain peace so that we can reflect when we are surrounded by other people. It is imperative that you are able to spend that time alone so that you can actually get that inner peace. If you want to be happy overall, you need to have the time to relax alone and recharge. You need to be able to spend that time figuring out what it is that you want. It is not only just that you want that time spent alone so that you can recharge—but you also need to be able to think and act accordingly.

Spend Time in Nature

Likewise, spending time in nature is imperative if you want to be happy as an empath. Most empaths find that nature is highly recharging for them. Nature is healing—we are meant to be outdoors, and in order to be happy, empaths require that connection to it in the first place. Being able to take a break from reality and modernity to be present with the plants and animals around is incredibly soothing, and empaths need it to be happy.

Some empaths cope with their need for nature by making sure that they spend time with their own pets. Some will set up home offices or other spaces with the use of all sorts of plants that can help them to feel that connection. Others will make it a point to garden on a regular basis. Others still may prefer to go hiking regularly, away from life. This is healthy for just about anyone—but the empaths, in particular, tend to benefit the most from such activities. You need that peace and quiet. You need the ability to ensure that you are recharging in nature, where you really belong.

If you play your cards right, you can make sure that you interact accordingly. You can spend your time soaking in the healing effects of nature, and the more that you do so, the happier that you will become. If you want to achieve true peace, you must be willing to accommodate accordingly, and that means that you must be willing to spend that time in private in nature, letting it heal you into the healthiest, happiest version of you that you can be.

Have Meaningful Conversations

To be happy, despite being an introvert, you will find that you need meaningful conversations. While introverts are people who are highly drained by interaction, they still enjoy being able to have deep conversations with others. People love being able to interact, and even the introvert is still a social animal—we need connection with others. We crave it, even when we feel like it may destroy us. Without that connection, it is difficult to be able to properly be happy in life.

Introverts, like anyone else, will get lonely at some point. They need to have that connection with other people if they want to be happy, and you must be able to get that somehow. For many people, that comes from deep, meaningful conversations. There is no reason to waste time with small talk for the empath— and most empaths find it too draining to tolerate in the first place.

With that in mind, you can see why it becomes imperative to ensure that you are always taking care to find other people that you can have those deep conversations with. Find people that can relate to you that understand what you mean when you want to talk about what matters. Find people who are interested in those discussions about how you should interact or why you should do things a certain way. Find people who like to find out what is on your mind or who want to philosophize about the world with you. It will help you to maintain that happiness.

Spare Yourself from Negative People

Of course, one of the easiest steps that any empath can take to help themselves to maintain positivity and happiness is to make sure that you avoid the negative people in your life. There is literally no reason to keep them around—people known commonly as energy vampires. They are the people who are simply exhausting to be around. When it comes right down to it, they are going to be one of the biggest barriers to happiness just by virtue of the way that they work— the energy vampires in your life are there just to leave you feeling exhausted.

They sense that you want nothing more than to help and heal those around you, and they take advantage of it. They see it as a weakness, as something that is worthy of being taken advantage of, and they will do anything in their power to ensure that they come out ahead. People who want to drain you will do so repeatedly and unabashedly as soon as they realize that they have found that in with you.

The best protection that you can have, then, make sure that you avoid those negative, toxic people. When you find that you are constantly being drained by the same people over and over again, feeling like you cannot continue to cope with the interactions much longer, you may be in the presence of an energy vampire. Do they regularly make you do things that you do not want to? Do they pressure you into certain behaviors, knowing that you will give in because they want you to? These are signs that you are near an energy vampire, someone who you should be avoided as much as possible to protect yourself from that sheer exhaustion and drain. You will be so much happier if you do.

Have Partners Who Are Supportive

You should also make sure that in your relationships, you prioritize one fact above all—supportiveness. You want your partners that you have in life to be supportive of you. They should understand what it is to be in a relationship with you. They need to be able to recognize what matters—that you need to ensure that you are taken care of.

It is difficult to be in a relationship as an empath—when you live with someone else, you will find that the entire time that you are with them, you are going to be exposed to someone else's energy. That means that your mind is constantly on overdrive, processing the feelings of other people, and trying to find a way to cope with them. This is difficult for the best of us—it is hard to be able to really focus on yourself when you are feeling the emotions of everyone else first, and because of that, you need to be able to figure out how to cope accordingly.

This means that if you want to be in a happy relationship, you need to be with someone who understands that you need that time to relax and get away. You need to be able to take time to yourself without offending your partner. You need to find someone else who can recognize that your boundaries, physical and personal, will be different from someone who is not highly sensitive.

Practice Mindfulness

When it comes to ensuring that your time and space are recognized and respected, you need to be able to practice mindfulness. Mindfulness should start first thing in the morning and continue around the clock. Everything that you do should be done in the name of mindfulness. Mindfully begin your day. Mindfully go about your day. Mindfully calm yourself down at the end of the day before you go to bed.

Mindfulness is the key to empath happiness—when you are mindful, you can start to better identify when the emotions that you are feeling are your own or when they are those of the other people that you are surrounded by. This means that if you want to be happy and able to succeed in your life, you must be able to see the ways that you interact with other people. You must be able to see when being around people starts to change the emotions that you are feeling as well.

With mindfulness, you can begin to understand the difference between where you end and where everyone else begins—this is imperative if you want to be able to control yourself and that happiness of yours as well. It is not always easy, but an investment in learning to be mindful will go a long way in attaining that long-term happiness for yourself if you know what you are doing.

Acceptance

Acceptance is highly important as an empath. It can be difficult to put up with the emotions running high. It can be tempting to attempt to fight off those emotions somehow or to try to avoid the problem altogether in other ways. However, if you play your cards right, you can learn to *accept*. This does not mean that you have to simply roll over and take anything that comes your way—rather, you will be learning to make the changes that you can when you can, while still accepting that sometimes, it is what it is and you will have to find a way to cope with that.

Acceptance matters greatly—you need to accept that your feelings will sometimes be running a bit haywire. You need to accept that sometimes, your way of interacting with others is not the preferred method for you. You need to accept that sometimes, your emotions *will* get the best of you, but you still need to find a way that you will be able to interact long-term. You need to be able to accept your ability while still making sure that you take steps to control it so that you are not entirely overwhelmed by them.

Peace and happiness are attained by this through being able to control the way that you respond. You are learning that you may not be able to control your emotions, but you can learn to control the way that you respond to them. You can learn to take away that lack of control over the emotions that you are feeling just by making sure that you know that they do not have to rule over you.

Hobbies

Hobbies are an essential part of any person's life, no matter what they are. Do you want to make crazy fan videos of your favorite songs being played with you tapping away at random objects around you? You can do that! Do you want to create miniature models of all of your favorite foods out of clay? Great! No matter what your hobbies are, if they bring you that happiness that you want or need, that is enough for you.

There is no rule that hobbies have to be useful—but they should bring you joy. If they do not bring you joy, then they are probably not a hobby by definition. You need to make sure that you have areas of your life that you enjoy. Yes, being an adult can be dull sometimes, especially if you find that your job is draining. However, you need to figure out ways that you can allow yourself to enjoy yourself.

What is it that matters the most to you? Do you enjoy making music? Do you like to write? Even if you happen to have been fortunate enough to turn your hobby into your career, you still need time to work on projects for yourself as well. You must be able to find that time for yourself so that you can be happy as well.

Self-Compassion

Finally, every empath alive needs self-compassion. It is, so hardtop be kind to oneself when you feel like you are at fault for everything that has happened. You need to learn how you can be kind to yourself. Whether you like it or not, you are an empath for life. There is no way that you can completely erase those tendencies—you need to be able to be kind to yourself for it. The sooner that you can accept what it is that you are as an empath, the sooner you can be kinder to yourself.

Self-compassion also requires you to be kind to yourself in other ways as well. Make sure that you are regularly taking care of what you need when you need it. If you know that you are tired, take a mental health break. Take the time that you will need to stop and unwind. Figure out ways that you are able to meet your needs. Forgive yourself when you make mistakes.

Empaths are already highly sensitive by nature. There is no reason that you should make it worse because you are upset with yourself. Take the time to forgive yourself and love yourself. The self-compassion will take you far in life if you want to be truly happy.

Chapter 6: Virtues in Stoicism

The Stoics of ancient Greece recognized four key virtues within their philosophy. They focused on what they referred to as prudence, justice, fortitude, and temperance. These four virtues were believed to be the goals of the philosophical ethics of the time. These four virtues defined what we all ought to work toward if we want to be happy in life. Stoicism was no exception—they looked toward these four virtues to guide them.

These four virtues will guide everything that you do in life if you were to live the Stoic lifestyle. To be a Stoic, you must make these virtues the key to everything that you do. They ought to guide you through every aspect of your life so that you know what you are doing. They should drive you forward, to keep you actively striving to achieve that happiness— Eudaimonia in the Greek understanding of ethics.

Within this chapter, we are going to take a closer look at the history of the Stoics and their teachings, understanding the points that they were trying to make when they did to get that better understanding of what it means to live the Stoic life. We are going to take a look at the role of virtue in ethics before finally addressing the four virtues that were believed to be the guiding forces in ancient Greek ethics.

A Closer Look at Stoicism

Before we begin, stop, and consider one point: Stoicism is not simply a way of thinking or a type of knowledge. Rather, philosophy, with Stoicism included, is a lifestyle. It is a way to live—it is exercises and practicing a specific type of life because you believe that it is the right one without any room for disagreement. Usually, philosophies of all kinds have their own justifications for why they matter and why they ought to be regarded as the right one. For Stoicism, we have the virtues justifying and validating its existence.

Stoicism is believed to begin in Plato's *Sophist,* in which he asks for some sort of indication for what is real in life, or what is existing in the moment. One of the answers that is considered is that being able to act or be acted upon is what marks us as being existent. Essentially, that is anything that can be acted upon or can act itself.

For the Stoics, this was accepted—however, they added to it. In the Stoic perspective, only bodies exist. Bodies can act or be acted upon, and therefore, they exist. They disregard the idea of materialists or spiritualists, instead choosing to specify that all that exists is the physical body itself. However, despite the fact that that which is, is limited specifically to the physical body, they recognize that there is also room for spirit as well.

That spirit, however, is created as energy, so to speak—it is the combination of the elements—fire, air, water, and earth. The active elements, in particular, fire and air, can create the pneuma—the spirit. The pneuma is believed to sustain the body and growth. Pneuma is what keeps us rooted, keeps us what we are physically. Of course, this is just barely breaching the surface of Stoicism and the arguments behind it.

Stoicism, as we know it today, comes from some of the followers of this philosophy. In particular, Marcus Aurelius became one of the greatest proponents of this type of thinking—he showed that he could possess the virtues that we will be discussing shortly and used those virtues to rule better than any other, according to historians.

Marcus Aurelius is commonly referred to as the last of the Five Good Emperors during the time in which the Roman Empire was ruled through wisdom and virtue—and we get a glimpse into his virtue through reading his *Meditations*. Stoicism became his way of life. The stony exterior, the stolid nonreactive traits, helped him to thrive as an emperor. It helped him to deal with stress as it inundated him, and he was able to rule one of the most influential, powerful nations that the world has ever seen.

The Virtues

Virtue is defined as being of the best disposition—it is a state in which someone is acting in ways interpreted to be good or true—they are observing the laws justly and ensuring that the individual is living as well as he or she can. Virtue is difficult to define—and the definition will vary greatly from person to person, from dictionary to dictionary, and from culture to culture. However, one thing holds true, no matter what—virtues are desirable. They are those traits that we ought to strive toward. They are the traits that aid us in figuring out what it is that society values from us so that we can be good and true. To be virtuous is to be just; it is to be adherent to those values that matter the most.

In Stoicism, the end goal from living the virtuous life is to achieve Eudaimonia—a state in which you can achieve utter happiness or fulfillment. It is the good that is created of all goods—the ability to live well and to be perfect in regard to virtue. Effectively, it is being able to live a good, true life with regard to the world around you, to be willing and able to follow the rules and considerations of the world that are the most important of all.

The virtues were seen as a way to control their passions. Passions ought to be avoided—fear, lust, distress, and delight ought to be feelings that are avoided. They cloud the mind; they prevent you from making decisions that matter the most, and because of that, it is important to avoid the passions. Passion, while acceptable today as something that is laudable is something that ought to be avoided, according to the Stoics. If life is all about living virtuously, passion is the greatest threat to exactly that. The virtues are the antidote to passion—they will allow for the individuals to live the virtuous, happy, rational life that they wish to lead all by clearing out those passions and preventing them from taking control.

Within Stoicism, it is believed that passion cannot enter the mind without the permission of the individual. Reason is what invites passion in, and is also what clears it out. Reason, then, becomes one's own worst enemy if it is not truly forged into what it ought to be, and that is where the rational, virtuous life comes into play. The virtues of life can teach the individual to fight back those traits. It can teach the individual to hold back those passions and prevent them from taking a stronghold over the individual's life, allowing them to effectively create the life that they want to live. Effectively, passion will be prevented through honing rationality through the use of virtues.

In terms of Stoicism itself, there are four key cardinal virtues that matter the most. These four virtues will guide the Stoic through life accordingly, teaching him or her everything that they need to know if they want to thrive. Let's take some time to get to know each of these key virtues.

Prudence or wisdom

The first that we will look at is wisdom or prudence—you will see it translated as either of these two words. It is the ability by which human happiness can be produced. It is the knowledge of good and bad, the knowledge that will help you to achieve happiness because of that knowledge. It will help us judge that which must be done and which we must not. Prudence, then, is the idea of moral wisdom—it is the most important of the virtues.

When living by wisdom or prudence, you must make sure that you are living a life with a full grasp of the situation. You understand that ultimately, the way that you interact with the world is dependent upon the ways in which you engage with those around you. It is dependent upon what is good or bad in life. You need to understand right and wrong, and that is done through prudence.

It is to understand the value of logic and reason. You choose the right thing to do, no matter how difficult it is for you because it is simply the right thing to do. It is this concept that you will not be attempting to make decisions based on emotions, but based on what makes the most sense at any given time. To live with prudence is to live with reason and logic, making it one of the most compelling of the points that are pushed within Stoicism.

It also refers to our ability to judge or weigh the value of things in the world rationally—with indifference. It is essential to being able to respond to the world around us in accordance with their values. If something is upsetting to you, for example, but is not actually important, all things considered, you must be able to let it go. This will help you to identify what matters the most and what you should be acting upon.

Justice or morality

Next comes the idea of justice or morality. Keep in mind that the translation to justice is a bit narrower than what is believed to be intended by the original Stoics—to refer to justice is so much more than just legal. It encompasses moral justice, as well. Justice refers to the unanimity of the soul itself—recognizing the discipline of the parts of the soul to create a law-abiding individual, an individual who treats their peers with value and justice. It is to obey the laws, but also to obey what matters morally speaking as well.

It is to treat people with fairness and kindness, along with that idea of justice; it is meant in the sense of social virtue rather than strictly legal. Marcus Aurelius states that justice is the most important of the virtues, recognizing that without justice, without that feeling of kindness or camaraderie with those around you, you can never truly interact appropriately or accordingly with those around you and the world itself as a society will struggle, or even fail.

Justice is the idea that moral wisdom is applied to the actions that we perform—it takes that understanding of what is and is not right and then applies that to action. It is to act with wisdom, effectively, to ensure that you are treating the people around you fairly. It is to approach the world with impartiality, meaning that you do not give anyone any preferential treatment in how you engage with them, and through kindness or courtesy.

Temperance or moderation

Next, we take a look at moderation or temperance. This is being able to regulate one's own reactions to the world around you; it is to be able to recognize that there is a line between wants and needs and that we must be able to control that line, to tow it, and to not give in hedonistically. It is wrong, according to the Stoics, for us to give in to something simply because we want it. Effectively, we ought to deny ourselves that which we do not rationally need—it is admirable to give yourself what you need but not to be ruled by your pleasures and what you may want, even if you cannot quite have it.

Think of temperance as mindfulness—it is being able to be self-aware so that you do not let your emotions get the best of you. You ought to be self-disciplined enough, for example, to prevent yourself from acting in ways that will be pleasant now but will not be good for you in the future. Effectively, you ought to be conscious of what you need and what you can avoid. Impulses, the desire to give in to certain wants, ought to be withheld. In Stoicism, moderation is pushed and defined as good self-discipline.

This is where that detached nature of the Stoic comes into play—when you are stoic, you are able to get that objective representation—that ability to deny yourself any desire or fear that may otherwise cloud your judgment. You are able to figure out what it is that you need to do through an objective lens, meaning that you will be able to make a better judgment over the whole situation.

Think about it—when you are emotional, are you thinking clearly? Despite the fact that so many of us would assert that yes, even in emotional states, they are thinking clearly, this is not actually the case. Remember, emotions are there to influence the way that you behave. They are influential by nature—that influence means that you are not going to be thinking clearly or rationally; you are guided by the emotions that you are feeling.

In Stoicism, however, the obvious answer is to let go of those emotions, stopping them from being able to entirely influence the individual in ways that are less than savory. If you want to be able to make those clear, dispassionate judgments, you must be able to achieve that freedom from unhealthy passions that will otherwise cloud your mind.

Fortitude or courage

Finally, the last virtue is fortitude or courage. This is being unmovable. To be courageous is to be able to behave without fear guiding you. It is to have that strict confidence in yourself—the knowledge that you have all of the facts and that you can use them. It is being restrained, about recognizing that you can withhold that fear that you may have facing something. It is being able to stand face to face with a terrible threat, something that is horrifying, and remain clear thinking in the moment. It is being able to balance out that fear and sense of danger with a sense of calmness—of being able to protect the soul, to ensure that you are feeling confident enough to take on anything that comes your way.

To have fortitude is to be calm. It is to be rational. It is to be able to persevere, even when all looks bleak. It is effectively to be courageous—but it goes a step further with Stoicism. Beyond just being courageous, Stoicism also recognizes that it is imperative to also be able to fight back—to be able to recognize that pain and discomfort must be endured as well. Through being fortitudinous, you are able to endure, and through endurance, you are able to keep a clearer mind, so that you are able to master yourself and the passions that you have.

Effectively, those who are courageous or fortitudinous are able to endure—they are able to conquer their fears or pains that they are suffering from. They are able to see the ways that they must interact, to recognize that at the end of the day, they must maintain control. It is only then that they are able to achieve the success that they want or need. When you are able to endure, you are able to renounce that control that pain or fear would have over you.

Of course, to be fortitudinous requires that there is that fear somewhere. You cannot conquer and deny your fear if there is no fear to conquer or deny. This is paradoxical, and yet, perfect by design. To be able to be virtuous, you must be able to recognize moderation in the first place. To have the virtues, you must also have the vices to defeat. Stoicism is not seeking the abolishment of those vices; rather, it is seeking to overcome them despite their presence to become a better individual; to become someone that is able to be virtuous in nature.

Chapter 7: The Stoic Life Is the Good Life

The Stoic life is one of simplicity; it is to be able to live your life on reason rather than going through life as an animal, allowing your impulses and feelings to drive you. Think about it—humankind has been given a gift, whether by design or by evolution. We are able to think rationally. We can overcome the temptation to engage with the world around us entirely emotionally. We can hold ourselves back when we feel that temptation to act passionately. When you can prevent yourself from those behaviors that are harmful, you know that you are able to live a life in which you are able to be true to the virtues that Stoicism advocates for.

When it comes to living a Stoic life, you are able to live a life of quiet simplicity; you are not complicating your life with emotions or irrationality. You are able to live a life that will help toward ensuring that you are constantly attempting to become your best self. You will constantly work to strive for what really matters the most—a life in which you are able to do everything that it is that matters to you.

Of course, to live the Stoic life is not always easy. It takes time to live the Stoic life, to truly reject the passions in favor of the virtues. It is difficult to let go of those emotions that control you and prevent you from working the way that you should be. It is difficult to figure out how you should and should not engage with the world, but in this chapter, you will see what needs to be done to live that life.

If you want a good, simple life, you must follow these steps. To be Stoic is to practice changing your life; it is to recognize that you can always do better, that you can always find new perspectives to follow, and that you are able to defeat your passions so that you can become someone better. You can reject the childish attitudes that you may be embodying by learning to better yourself, and in doing so, you bring yourself closer to success than ever.

Control the Thinking

To begin with your Stoic training, you must recognize that you need control. According to Epictetus, one of the original Stoics, you must make sure that you are in control of what you can be. Ultimately, according to Epictetus, you cannot control very much in the world. You have no sway over the people around you, for example—you can influence them, but influence is not the same as genuine control.

They are not something that you can force into behaving a certain way on a whim in the sense that you can control your foot and make it move. You cannot control the world around you entirely. You cannot even totally control yourself—you cannot choose when you will get sick or when you will be injured, for example. So, then, what can you control, you may ask?

You can control your thoughts. The one thing in this great big world that you can control is your thoughts. This is imperative to remember—when you control your thoughts, you control the way that you engage with the world around you. Thoughts will influence feelings and feelings will influence behaviors, and the sooner that you develop an understanding and an affinity for this fact, the sooner that you can ensure that you live the Stoic life that you have always wanted to set out and enjoy. Think about it this way—when you think positively, you feel positive. When you feel positive, you tend to behave positively, as well.

Because you can control your thoughts on a whim, you can effectively make sure that no matter what, you are in the right mindset. This means that you can reject the negative emotions that will try to control you. You can remind yourself that you are not behaving logically if such a time were to arise. You can make sure that you are regulating yourself so that you can trust that you are making the right decisions. If you can do that, you can control yourself.

Try this for a week: Every single time that you have a negative thought, remind yourself that you ought to be thinking positively—and enforce it.

Keep in mind that this does not mean that you should reject any emotionality that you have—emotions are there for a reason! They are like warning flags, letting us know what is going on around us. However, you should also make sure that if something is happening around you, you are able to override those negative emotions. You can prevent them from being able to control you or make you do something that you are going to reject.

Emotions are ultimately the product of the judgments that we make—if you realize that the judgments that you are making are actually becoming problematic for you for some reason, you can reject the idea entirely. You can redirect and correct yourself so that you can protect yourself. If you can do this, you can make sure that ultimately, you are able to make the right judgments that ultimately will matter more than anything else. You can be happy if you can alter those judgments. Stoicism is paradoxical in the sense that you have control over next to nothing, and yet you have unlimited control over the happiness that you can attain.

Train the Mind

Next, if you want to live the Stoic life, you must train your mind as much as you can. This means that you must work to understand the world around you. You must think differently if you can. You must make sure that you consider the positions of other people as well. If you think differently, you can start to see perspectives that you may not have realized the first time around. You may wonder whether or not the behaviors that you complete actually matter. They do, in fact—you can acknowledge other perspectives, and in doing so, you can ensure that you are learning more.

Stoics work to train their minds—they stop and look at the world and the life that they lived for the day. They consider whether or not there was anything that ultimately was not particularly important that led to annoyance or irritation, and if there was something, how that can be avoided in the future. This process of constant self-reflection allows for the Stoics to constantly be training their minds, shielding themselves against the negativity that they may otherwise face. When this is done properly, it aids in making sure that you are making better decisions every day.

It is impossible for any of us to be perfect—there is no way that you will ever get every last moment of your life just right. However, what you can learn to do is figure out what it is that you did wrong today so that tomorrow, you can do better. The sooner that you embrace this, the sooner that you can succeed.

You can also start each and every day that you will almost definitely encounter people that you will dislike throughout the day. Someone will do something that is going to frustrate you. Someone will seem ungrateful. You will find that ultimately, you will be unhappy at some point—but you can learn to control it. You can learn to choose happiness. You can learn to reflect that most of those people that you will encounter are not inherently frustrated at you— rather, they are probably unintentionally upset, a slave to their own passions and judgments. You can choose not to add to that by refusing to be moved by them.

Practice Acceptance

Similarly to being able to practice training the mind, you can make sure that you are able to accept that things are what they are. One important fact to keep in mind is that the world is not circling around you. The world does not care about you. The world does not care that ultimately, you are behaving a certain way—most people probably do not even know who you are anyway. However, when you accept that your position in the world is one of unimportance, you can start to accept that the context of what you do is inconsequential. The universe is not going to give you what you want just because you want it—because you *are* inconsequential. You can embrace what the universe does give you, however.

To practice acceptance is to recognize that while you cannot control what happens around you, you can accept it and then control the way that you respond. When you are able to control the way that you engage with the world, you can find that ultimately, you become the gatekeeper to your own happiness. You cannot get upset over something going wrong when you simply accept that things are what they are, and there is little that you can do about it.

By changing your attitude instead of trying to fight against something that you have no control over, you can ensure that you are in control. Despite the paradox, this is the perfect way for you to maintain that happiness that you need if you want to thrive as a Stoic.

Practice Minimalism

Another key practice of Stoicism is to relinquish the idea that you must have everything to be happy. According to Epictetus, *"Wealth consists not in having great possessions, but in having few wants."* Effectively, you are not wealthy if you have everything around you but still want more—than the desire for more and more materialistic goods is only going to drag you down further. It is only going to make it harder for you to achieve that true happiness that you were looking for. Rather than allowing yourself to be eaten up by that materialistic nonsense, Stoicism encourages the renouncement of needing constant materialistic justifications.

Instead of constantly seeking out more and more items around you, you should be paying closer attention to what you have. You do not need the latest and greatest iPhone to be happy. You do not need

$1,000,000 in the bank to be happy. What you need, however, is the people in your life that you love.

Remember, Stoicism is not about renouncing emotions—it is about renouncing being enslaved by them. You are allowed to love people in Stoicism. You are allowed to find that there are people that you care deeply about. They are who matter in your life. Being able to strive toward happiness requires you to want less—it requires you to find that happiness through being satisfied with what you have.

Practice Gratitude

Of course, being able to be satisfied with what you have requires you to practice gratitude. When you are grateful for the world that you live in and the people in it, you are able to be happier. This also helps you stop yourself from constantly seeking to get more around you. Life is not about dreaming of having what you currently lack—it is about being able to see that you should be thankful for what you have.

Think about it for a moment, if the people that you loved the most in life were suddenly to disappear, what would you do? How would you feel if suddenly, you were without your best friend? Your children? Your spouse or significant other? You would probably be devastated to lose them—but do you appreciate them in the moment?

We take for granted the people around us all too often. We assume that they will be there regardless of what happens, and that could not be further from the truth. The truth of the matter is that we treat everyone as if they are given rather than a luxury. We have the luxury of knowing those people around us. We have the luxury of having our friends, family, and children. They are a blessing—and it is difficult for many people to accept this. We take what we have for granted.

Every now and then, practice imagining what you would do if you suddenly found yourself without. Walk to work instead of driving. Leave your phone at home for a day. Spend a day not engaging with those that you love. It is an exercise in seeing what you have. Ultimately, we oftentimes find that we do not miss what we have until it is gone.

However, as a Stoic, you owe it to yourself to recognize what you have. You owe it to yourself to recognize the truth of the matter—that what you have matters immensely and that what you have ought to be honored and cherished even though you have it.

Be Kind and Cheerful

Remember, one of the virtues was to be just to people around you—you ought to treat people fairly and kindly. The idea of justice was more along the lines of treating people kindly and fairly, a sort of social virtue. It is important for you to be kind to those around you. It is imperative to recognize that happiness that we have comes from human experience.

The greatest joys that we have of all are our inner joys—those that we can delight in within ourselves without having to purchase something or do something that encourages those feelings. It is imperative to recognize this; to live by the idea that at the end of the day, we must be kind to ourselves, and also to those around us.

By being kind to those around you, you are providing other people with the goodness from your hearts. Goodness spread throughout the world is what will help the world continue to progress. Your goodness into the world will help you to advance society, and that is fulfilling on its own. Even better, it costs you nothing to be kind to those around you.

Practice What You Preach

Finally, remember that at the end of the day, living what you say is important to you is the best thing that you can do. It is not enough to simply voice that you believe something—you must also live it. Think about it—you could say that you are all for banning plastic bottles as you sip at a plastic water bottle. Is that really something that you care about if you are voicing that you want to do so as you are sitting there, using one?

To practice what you preach shows conviction; it shows that you actually do care about what you are saying. You must make sure that you always do this— you must practice what you preach so that people show that you are serious. When you do not, you come across as pretentious, or like you are only saying something because you want the credit for something that you honestly do not care about. It is not enough for you to voice something. You must act, and Stoicism regularly pushes for this.

In Stoicism, you are obligated to act in ways that are going to be true to your own personal philosophies, no matter what they are. When you are practicing Stoicism, it is expected of you to ask yourself how you can act in any given moment and if that particular choice is really the right one for you, given the context. When you are able to live the right kind of life with the right kinds of decisions, you can usually show everyone around you that you are, in fact, dedicated to the morals and values that you have been advocating for.

Ultimately, then, Stoicism as a practice is meant to be something that you can use to control the way that you engage with the world around you. It is meant to guide you to better your life. It is to work to better yourself, to ensure that you live a life that matters to you. When you can do that, when you can make sure that the life that you live is one that matters the most to you, you can ensure that the life that you live is one that is valuable.

You owe it to yourself to better yourself. You owe it to yourself to make sure that you do not allow yourself to get entirely caught up in materialism. You must make sure that you always try to engage with other people in the best ways possible. You ought to make sure that what you do is going to aid in bettering the world. To live the good Stoic life is to live the life in which you do not let the world around you that is out of your control overwhelm you. It is imperative that the life that you live is one that you will be able to control everything. If there is one takeaway on what the proper Stoic life is, it is that you have control over the way that you react and when you can acknowledge that, you can get far.

Chapter 8: Stoicism and Emotions

Though it is used otherwise often in writing, Stoicism is not to be emotionless. Make sure that you get that thought out of your mind. To be Stoic is not to be emotionless—it is to be nonreactive. However, the two are not the same thing, despite the fact that many people would believe otherwise. Stoicism is not about repressing emotions. It is about feeling. It is about striving for Eudaimonia—for that joy in life in which you are able to control yourself and your reactions. The sooner that you can achieve that state of Eudaimonia, the happier you will be.

This means that Stoics, then, are emotional by nature. Of course, they are—they are people just like anyone else, and people are living, emotional beings. People seem to think of them as unemotional, but in reality, to be a Stoic is to be constantly striving to be the best human that you can be—emotions and all. This means that you have no choice but to accept those emotions for what they are. You have to make sure that you are embracing those emotions, that you are embracing the idea of who you are and what you want. The sooner that you can embrace humanity, the sooner that you can get on the right track.

To be Stoic is to live according to nature. This challenges the Stoics; it encourages us to constantly figure out what our place in the universe is. What are we? How do we exist? Are we real? Are we able to prove that we are real? What does it matter if we are? These are questions that matter to the Stoic—it becomes imperative to recognize that ultimately, the way that you engage with the world around you is important, and that is done through emotions.

Of course, the approach to emotional life for the Stoics is a bit different than most would consider. Rather than being in touch with all emotions and letting them run rampant, Stoics look to control themselves. They approach their emotions as being just that—impulsive feelings. They are like the weather, so to speak; rather than something that ought to be treated as reliable or dependable, or even predictable, they should be seen as natural occurrences that will cause us to make changes to our behavior.

Think about it—you change your behavior based on the weather. You may wear different clothes. You may wear sunglasses if the sun is shining or if it has snowed and created a massive amount of glare. If it is hot out and sunny, you will probably put on sunscreen. If the roads are icy, you will probably slow down. Your emotions are much like these storms— they will constantly influence your mind and your actions, and that is what the Stoics tend to address.

The Stoics see that your emotions are highly volatile. They see that it is possible for your emotions to rule you and to try to drag you into behaving in certain ways that may not be appropriate—and they then decide to control it. Rather than giving in to those behaviors, the Stoics learn to weather the storm—they learn what they can do to prevent those emotions from taking control over the whole situation. They prevent themselves from being able to be flooded by those emotions that will otherwise cause them to behave to other people in negative manners.

Ultimately, emotions matter to the Stoic. They become guiding factors in just about every point of the Stoic's life, and because of that, it becomes imperative to judge accordingly. You must make sure that you are engaging with the world around you as well as you can, and that means being able to control the emotions that you are putting out, or at the very least, controlling the reactions to the emotions that you have.

There are ultimately three positive emotions that are identified by the Stoics and three negative ones as well. These emotions guide just about everything in life, according to Stoics. You have the good emotions of joy, wish, and caution, along with the three passions, the negative emotions of pleasure, appetite or lust, and fear. Of course, if you are unfamiliar with Stoicism, you are probably scratching your head right now, trying to figure out the difference between the two. It is slight, but it is there, and the sooner that you learn the differences, the sooner that you can understand the emotional states of the Stoic.

When you recognize the differences between the two, you start to see those small subtleties that matter—the technicalities upon which the two are so similar, and yet able to be entirely separated out from each other. When it comes right down to it, the most important thing to remember is that there is a good and a bad emotion for everything.

Keep in mind that these emotions that you are being given will encompass all others as well. These are the overarching categories on either side, and everything else will sort of funnel into one of the six given.

The Stoics and Joy Versus Pleasure

First comes joy versus pleasure. Joy and pleasure are not inherently the same, despite what many people would think. In Stoicism, there is an emphasis on finding joy rather than the passion of pleasure. When you recognize the difference between the two, you will start to understand what matters more.

Joy is happiness that is not dependent upon what happens. No matter what happens in that situation, you will still have joy. Think about it this way—have you ever heard the expression that a bad pizza is still good? Sure, a bad pizza is probably going to be disappointing if you thought that you were in the market for something better. However, most of the time, even a bad pizza, so long as it is not burnt or rotten with normal toppings on it, is going to still be good. It is hard to mess up pizza, and you will probably still enjoy it to some degree or another.

Pleasure, however, is dependent upon the outcome. It is dependent upon what may come next to make things happen. Pleasure happens when you enjoy what the end result is. You may find pleasure in, for example, winning some money on your scratch ticket. If asked if you find that gambling with scratch tickets is pleasurable, you may say yes—but the answer is that it is really only pleasurable when you win. Otherwise, it is frustrating and honestly feels like a waste of money. When you recognize this difference, you start to see the truth—joy is virtuous and pure. Pleasure is hedonistic.

Hedonists are seen as the opposite of Stoics oftentimes—in hedonism, the idea is that pleasure is deemed the highest form of good that exists. It is important to maximize pleasure, to enjoy what is happening as much as possible to ensure that you are happy. To be good is to be pleasurable. However, in Stoicism, that emotionality and that cling to pleasure are actually seen as problematic. It is not pleasure that is desired, argue the Stoics, but rather, the joy that they get through doing the right thing.

Think for a moment, then, about what makes something enjoyable—many people will say that it feels good or it seems like the right thing to do. To feel joy is to feel morally sound. It is to feel as if you are being true to the virtues that you value. When you are able to be joyous about something, you recognize that you are happy no matter what happens—you have made the right moral decision because of that.

The Stoics and Wish Versus Lust

Next comes the idea of wish versus lust or appetite. This particular dichotomy may seem strange as well— after all is a wish, not some degree of lust, or is lust, not a wish? However, there is an important distinguishing factor here—pining for things that you do not have, lusting over something that you cannot get, is greedy. If you are lusting over something, you are acting with greed.

Think about it—if you are sitting there, looking at an attractive person, wishing that you could have your way with them, are you thinking in a Stoic manner? You are being lustful in the literal sense of the word— you want something selfishly without regard for what the end result will be. If you decided to pursue the other person, even after the other person expressed being uninterested, you would be chasing after something irrationally in hopes of getting something good.

However, lust is taken one step further in Stoicism— you do not just lust after someone that you find attractive. Rather, you lust over anything that you want but cannot have, or that you do not have. It is that desire and waste of energy toward something that you hope to get despite knowing that it is unlikely Greed becomes that appetite, that lust, for material things. Of course, you can also lust after other things as well, such as lusting after revenge for something that has happened. If you are able to recognize that lust is something negative or problematic, you recognize that ultimately, no matter what happens, you are working against yourself. You are hurting yourself—you are wasting energy.

Wish, then, is a feeling of, "Wow, I really wish I had this thing, but I know that I do not need that to experience joy." You are allowed to want things—there are no rules against not wanting to get the newest phone after your old one shattered when you dropped it. You are welcome to get new things that you want—but remember that ultimately, those things that you want are not going to determine your happiness.

They will not bring you joy for the sake of having them—or rather, you will not feel an absence of joy if you do not get the item in the first place. When it comes right down to it, the emotions that you feel, the behaviors that you have, and more, are all based on whether you are acting in lust or in wish. You can wish for anything that you want, so long as you can make the distinction between wanting and needing something for your happiness.

The Stoics and Caution Versus Fear

Finally comes the idea of caution versus fear. Again, these may seem quite similar at first glance—is it not a bit pedantic to state that fear and caution are not the same? After all, whether you are cautious or afraid, you are going to be taking the same steps to avoid whatever it is that you believe is dangerous in that situation. It is important for you to recognize the truth—that there is some sort of defining difference between the two.

Remember that to feel fear does not make you weak. It does not mean that you are wrong—and there are some situations in which fear is entirely justifiable. However, you should also remember that ultimately, the way that you feel is something that you can influence.

Fear is defined as an irrational aversion. You expect that there is going to be some sort of danger, and you act accordingly. You believe that the threat will happen, and you start to plan. Of course, this comes at a major cost. Instead of being happy in the moment, you find that you are actually incredibly unhappy instead. You struggle to interact with the ways that you should be encouraged to behave. You struggle to act in ways that are going to be rational. You tell yourself that you are afraid that something will happen, so you have to take certain precautions.

Imagine this—you are suddenly convinced that you are due for a major earthquake in your area that is going to cause utter destruction across the population. You tell yourself that the earthquake is going to be so bad that food lines and other sorts of trade routes, which we need to survive, will be shattered, so you decide to stock up to the best of your ability to prevent yourself from being unprepared. You are terrified that the earthquake may come, and you do everything in your power to prepare, followed by living your life terrified that things are going to get worse. You keep yourself at home. You lock yourself away and refuse to go anywhere. You spend your day hiding under your desk, believing that at the very least, you will be safe under there if your roof collapses. This is fear.

In this example, you are afraid of something that may come at some point. You let go of your current joy that you could have in favor of letting the future potential negativity take it away. When it comes right down to it, the way that you engage with the world is entirely dependent upon the way that you view those concerns that you have.

On the other hand, if you behave with caution, you recognize that sometimes, life does something unpredictable or something that is going to be uncomfortable. However, instead of living underneath a desk and refusing to go out, you decide that you are going to prepare as much as you can. You make sure that everything that is important to you is sealed up. Furniture is secured to the walls so that it will not tip over in an earthquake. You make sure that any items that matter to you are secured so that they will not be destroyed.

You work hard to ensure that everything is as safe as possible, knowing that in doing so, you can protect yourself as much as possible. However, you refuse to change your life for a maybe. You refuse to sacrifice your current joy for potential dangers. The earthquake could be in 10 minutes or ten centuries—but you should be prepared anyway. In being cautious, you are able to approach with awareness. You understand that ultimately, it is important to plan accordingly and ensure that you are taking care of everything to the best of your ability.

Chapter 9: Finding Inner Peace

Peace of mind is the ultimate goal for most people. It is so great to find that peaceful point—that point in which you are certain that you have done everything that you can and attempted to live the right life for yourself. That point in which you are able to accept that you are living your best life and enjoying it. Think of the lucky few who have achieved this—they are calm. They are patient. They are able to deal with just about anything with kindness. Despite just how easy these people make it seem, these people must work hard to make this sort of emotional state occur.

To be at peace is highly demanding on the mind, contrary to popular belief. To be at peace requires you to be able to develop enough emotional control to not give in whenever something goes wrong. To be at peace is to ensure that you are able to succeed accordingly. It is to recognize that ultimately, the ways that you behave in life are dependent upon your mindset.

If you want to be at peace, Stoicism is for you. Stoic philosophers have been pursuing that degree of peace for centuries. Marcus Aurelius dedicated every morning to working with his journals. Epictetus constantly stated that men are disturbed by the thoughts that are developed rather than what happens around you. It is important for people to remember that ultimately, to be at peace is to be in control of the mind.

It is to be in control of the thoughts. Stoicism has endured for thousands of years and is still so popular because it allows for that degree of control that people want. It teaches people how they can begin to control themselves. It reminds them of what they need to do so that they can guide themselves throughout their own lives on the right paths. If you are able to develop that ability to behave Stoically, you can live a peaceful life.

Both Marcus Aurelius and Epictetus saw philosophy not as something to use every now and then, but as a way of life—they constantly revisited the philosophies they were studying. They regarded the philosophy of Stoicism as something that could be used to aid them in just about every aspect of life. They learned to become more reflective and less reactive. They turned inward instead of outward. They learned to keep their cool, to recognize that sometimes, the best thing that you can do in life is to simply let things go and move on.

When it comes right down to it, to be peaceful, to live your most successful, happiest life, you must embrace these concepts. You must let go of the idea that ultimately, you are stuck with your negativity or in the mindset that you are in. If you want to achieve inner peace yourself, there are steps that you can take to ensure that you make it happen. It may not be easy, but it is something that you can do for yourself. All you have to do is set out to make it happen. Within this chapter, we are going to look at the several steps toward finding inner peace as a Stoic. Live these ideas. Let them guide you and the life that you live. You will discover what matters the most in your life, and you will discover that you are all the happier for it.

Let Go of Anxiety

It is so easy to get caught up in the idea that things are far worse than they may seem, and the unfortunate reality is that as soon as you do that, you find yourself in a constant spiral in which you want to do better, but you cannot. You get yourself stuck in this mindset of being unable to manage the current situation that you are in because you are too busy catastrophizing to realize that things are not actually that bad in the first place.

We tend to be more afraid of all of the what-ifs rather than the realities of situations, and because of that, it becomes important to let go of them. Yes, this is easier said than done, but it is highly powerful. If you want to escape the anxiety that you have and live a Stoic life, you must be making it a point to engage with your life in the most beneficial way that you can muster. You must make sure that you work to provide yourself with everything that you know to be true. You must work to ensure that you are able to remind yourself that catastrophizing never helped anyone.

Remind yourself to stay in the moment—practice mindfulness. Refuse to allow your emotions that you are feeling rule the moment. Let yourself focus on the world around you in the moment and keep yourself there. Are things actually that bad? When you stop feeling so anxious all of the time, you can usually work to feel better and do better. If you want to feel at peace, you must make sure that you reject the idea of anxiety. Let yourself be who you are and let yourself only focus on the present problems.

Accept Mortality

It is so easy to get caught up in the idea of your impending death to the point that you tend to forget the truth of the matter—we all die at some point, and we will never know when that is. Ultimately, the only people that know when their death is, are those that are about to end them—at which point, they have already accepted their own mortality.

However, dwelling about your death, when it will happen, and what you can do to mitigate the death that will happen eventually will only cause you to miss out on what is happening in the moment. Instead of enjoying whatever is left of your life, you are finding yourself constantly worrying about what could go wrong. You may not go on that cruise because you are afraid that it will be a repeat of the Titanic. You will pass up that dream job because you think the extra 20 minutes per day of freeway driving puts your life at too much risk. Rational? Not really.

When you accept that you will die at some point and that there will be nothing that you can do about it when it happens, you can begin to remove some of that anxiety over it. You will be able to recognize that death will happen at some point, and in making peace, you can then work with trying to live the right kind of life. You can work to make sure that you are motivated to live each life to its fullest, to work to the best of your ability to live the best possible life that you can so that you do not die with regrets.

Your fear of death should be shifted into a motivation to do the most with what you have—as much as you can. This means that you need to work hard with yourself. This means that you must work to constantly follow what matters to you. You must make sure that you are engaging in the actions that matter the most to you. If that means that you are going to travel the world to volunteer time, then do it. If you are going to breed puppies, then do it. Life is short. Do not let it all pass by until you have none left to live.

Remember Whose Opinions Matter the Most

Perhaps one of the largest sources of anxiety that we have these days comes from the worry about what other people think about us. We all constantly worry about other people think about ourselves even though ultimately, we all tend to prioritize ourselves over other people. When it comes right down to it, the opinions of everyone around you are not as important as your own. When it comes right down to it, it is your opinion that matters the most, and when you recognize that and take that into consideration, you can start to erase some of those worries that you have.

Think about it—today, we are endlessly connected online. We are constantly able to get back to people quickly and easily. We are all constantly inundated with opinions, and if it is on the internet, everyone has one. However, ultimately, when it comes right down to it, the only opinion that truly matters is your own. It does not matter what your neighbor thinks about your haircut—what do you think about it?

Humans are social animals, and because we are, we worry about what other people think about us. However, in reality, there are so many different people in the world with so many different opinions and desires that if you were to try to consider every single person's opinion, you would never get anything done. Why, then, do you let the people that are in your immediate vicinity pass judgment?

Spending your life worrying about what everyone else thinks is only setting yourself up for feeling like you have to compete against others. It sets you up for the expectation of keeping up with the Joneses, and that is a huge problem—you doing so will remove just about any peace that you could have ever possibly attained all by virtue of the fact that you are now so worried about being seen as something that you may not be that you are not focusing on what matters.

Keep your focus on what matters—your own thoughts. Make sure that you live a life that makes you happy. Let go of the idea that you have to be liked by all.

Instead, focus on what you can do to be kind and disciplined. What can you do to master tolerance over pain and displeasure? How can you maintain your patience? These are what matter. Ultimately, as soon as you stop caring about what everyone around you thinks, you will find that you are far happier than you thought that you would be.

Take Time to Be Still

If peace is what you want to achieve, then you have to live it as well. If you want to be truly peaceful, then you have to schedule in the time to be at peace. Even in a rapidly evolving world, where we are constantly working on more and being busier than ever, it is imperative that you take the time to ensure that you are calm and able to remind yourself that ultimately, the way that you behave matters more than anything else. If you want to be able to interact with people in a calm manner, then you have to practice calmness.

Practicing peaceful stillness is a great way for you to really embody what you want out of life. Remember, you must always practice what you preach, and this is where you start. If you want to be calm, then be physically calm. Take some time each day to spend time in peace, in stillness, and in quiet. This means that every single day, you need to prioritize some time in which you are doing nothing. No phones. No television. No talking to other people. You will sit quietly and enjoy the moment. This is all about making sure that you get to know the peace that you want.

This is something that is difficult; however—we find that ultimately, it is impossible for people to stop and really reflect in the moment. You must be able to master this art—you must be able to remind yourself that ultimately, you need calmness in your life if you want to be successful in making sure that you are keeping up with your practice. The sooner that you can practice the calmness and stillness, the sooner that your mind will learn to reflect silently and peacefully.

Find the Beauty in Every Situation

Even though Stoicism pushes this idea that you ought to be unmoving, logical, and at peace, there is still enjoyment found within it. You should always take the time that you can to find the beauty that exists. There is beauty in just about anything—you just have to know where or how to look. If you can do that, if you can figure out how to look at a situation and see the beauty in it, you can live the Stoic life with ease.

Think about it—even in a storm; there is something to look forward to. The grass and plants are getting much-needed water that they will use to provide for themselves. The animals will have new puddles that can be used to drink from. The water is pure and clean. There may be a rainbow. The sound of rain is refreshing and beautiful on its own. The smell of petrichor, that first moment in which rain starts to fall.

Beauty is visible everywhere around you. Beauty can be found in even the darkest of places, and when you realize that even those things in the world that could be painful or difficult to deal with can have some beauty in them, even if that beauty is not yet apparent to you in the moment, it can become apparent to you in the future. You can learn what it is that matters. You can learn to recognize that beauty and respect it. You can discover what it will take for you to accept what has happened so that you can respond accordingly.

The next time that you are walking somewhere stop and consider the beauty of the blue sky. Enjoy the taste of the coffee that you are sipping instead of chugging it down to get that caffeine before rushing off. Stop and savor the feeling of hot water running down your back in the shower. It will be worth it.

Imagine a New Perspective

It is so easy to get caught up in the moment when something is going wrong. It is so easy to find that you are constantly worrying about the moment that you suddenly are missing something. You can get stuck in what you see in front of you—but really, what if you consider a different perspective? What if you imagined yourself from above the problem instead of beside it?

Think about it—imagine that your car just died. You are frustrated. However, if you were to stop and imagine it from a bird's perspective, the car would probably not even be a blip on its radar. You can move further up—from an airplane; you could not even see your broken-down car. Even higher, you may not be able to see your street or even your city.

The universe is immense. When you are feeling that emotions are running high, you can remind yourself of the insignificance of the moment. Why get so worked up over something that is not really that big after all? If you want to be in a mindset of peace, this is not how you achieve it. If you are not careful, you will find that you are not able to maintain that peace at all—you are going to be stuck in the negativity of the situation. The next time that you feel that you are upset try reimagining the situation. If you were to look at things from the top down, how significant would it be?

Follow Your Code

Stoicism creates a framework that we can live by—it is a list of guidelines that we can use to reflect upon the world and determine how we align ourselves with it. If you look at the way that you engage with the world through the lens of code, you remind yourself that ultimately, you have set behaviors that you want to follow. The code becomes a sort of way for you to determine what is good and what is bad.

This helps you to achieve that inner peace as a Stoic for one reason: It simplifies things. When you approach the situation as a Stoic, you know that you are working to avoid letting emotionality play a role in your decisions. You are looking at things as rationally and logically as you can because you hope that in doing so, you can make sure that you make the right choices. Rationality becomes your code, and that brings you peace. When you know your place and what is expected of you, it is easy to be in that position or state of peace, and you will not have to do much more to maintain it. Simply make sure that you are following your code and not violating it. If it is wrong, do not do it. Stand by your convictions. Follow your moral code of conduct. If you can do this, you will be at peace with yourself.

Reflect

Finally, if you wish to achieve inner peace, the most important of all is to reflect. Make sure that you reflect upon your days every single day. In particular, Stoics tend to prefer the art of journaling. It works well to allow you to gather your thoughts, to address why you did what you did. It allows you to think about how you can better yourself in the future, or what you can do if you want to change the interactions that you have with those in your area. Though you can ultimately reflect in any way that you want to, to reflect through journaling gives you a wonderful way through which you can make sure that you are documenting all of the details. This will ensure that you know that you did something a certain way and what the implications are.

To reflect is to observe. To reflect on what matters the most in your life, you are able to focus where it matters—on the ways that you should be interacting with people. On how you can stay true to yourself. You are able to reason with yourself so that you can continue to better yourself. Every single day, you will become more and more aware of yourself and your habits, and through becoming more aware, you will find that ultimately, you have made some major moves toward being the successful Stoic that you want to be. Remember, you are always a work in progress, and through journaling, you will bring yourself closer to that feeling of peace.

Chapter 10: Tips and Strategies on Finding the Right Balance Between Stoicism and Empathic Ways of Life

Stoicism and empathic ways of life are not directly separated from each other. There is no reason that a stoic cannot be empathic, or an empath cannot be stoic. In fact, combining the two together can actually help to create a much more level mindset that can aid both. Despite the fact that empaths are highly emotional and Stoics strive to be as emotionally in control as possible, they work well together—to learn to master both types of life is to ensure that you can live a life much more likely to be successful. If you want to be able to sort of find that middle ground, following that state of both empathy and stoicism is the perfect way to ensure that you are working with the people around you in ways that you know are going to benefit everyone involved.

It is not enough to simply admit one way or another that you are stoic or empathic. You must also make it a point to learn to hone your skills. You must learn how you can properly manage to control yourself and your emotions while also recognizing the truth of the matter: That you need to ensure that you can recognize your emotions.

Let's look back at the empath for a moment—most empaths struggle with being able to interact with other people for very long. The emotions that they feel tend to become too overwhelming, and they instead choose to not have to engage at all. However, that does not have to be the case. There is no reason that you have to engage as an empath. You can learn to reject those highly volatile emotions so that you can be more in control.

For the empath that is out of control and unable to manage how they feel, or who is constantly feeling overwhelmed, being able to stop and remind yourself of one thing—that you are able to engage with the world from a Stoic perspective, could be the change that you are looking for. Remember, the Stoics do not want to mute your emotions—they just want you to reflect upon them.

Within this chapter, we are going to go over some keys to being able to control yourself. We are going to take a look at how the empath can become Stoic, following those Stoic principles to avoid being entirely overwhelmed whenever emotions start to run high. If you know what you are doing, you can begin to take control; you can learn to be the person that you have always wanted to be. Now, let's take a look at what you can do to control yourself and become a Stoic Empath.

Develop Your Control

We do not control much in life at all. We have gone over this repeatedly. As an empath, you probably know this better than anyone—you cannot control the emotions when they run through you. However, you can control one thing: Your thoughts. We have asserted this. Epictetus was a slave—he was born into slavery and crippled when his master broke his leg. He lived in poverty and died there, too. However, despite the fact that he had no control over his body, he still controlled his thoughts.

Think about this as an empath for a moment—you may not control your feelings, but you can control your thoughts about them. You can remind yourself that you have no reason to get frustrated when you can take control of how you think. Through controlling your thoughts, you can change your reactions. Instead of getting stressed by emotions, you can remind yourself that ultimately, they are what they are, but they are not your feelings and therefore are none of your concern, so you should move on. When you can recognize that you can control your mind and thoughts, you will become much happier than you thought you could be.

Protect Your Time

We oftentimes are loose with our time. We waste it scrolling through social media or not doing anything important. However, unlike literally everything else in life, which we can get more of, time can never be reclaimed. You can make more money. You can buy more things. You can even make more children or remarry a new spouse. However, nothing that you do will ever turn back time.

Remember this. Protect your time from everyone around you. In particular, you must guard that time alone to recharge so that you know that you are able to properly cope with everything that you face in your life. If you want to be comfortable with yourself, you need to be able to control the way that you think or feel. If you want to live a life of happiness, you must be able to protect the time for yourself.

Recognize Happiness Is from Within

Remember that while you may act in ways that you do because you want to be accepted by those around you, true happiness is found within yourself. It does not come from external sources, such as how you engage with someone else or what you can do for them. True happiness is not dependent upon how other people choose to interact with you.

As an empath, it can be easy to give in to hope that other people will be happier with you or will like you more when you do so. However, you are under no obligation to give to other people to make them happy—in fact; you should avoid doing exactly that.

Make sure that you only work for internal happiness. Find that true Eudaimonia—that inner joy. It does not have to be outsourced. Other people are not responsible for making you happy, just like you are not responsible for their happiness.

Keep Your Focus

As an empath, it is easy to get distracted all around you with all of the noises and emotional pollution in the air. It is incredibly easy to get distracted in the moment, to give up trying to do something a certain way if you do not know what you are doing. It can be easy to get entirely sidetracked, to feel like if you do not do something a certain way, there will be a problem.

However, remind yourself that you can choose. You can learn to pick and choose what matters the most to you. You can figure out what it is that you want to do so that you can be successful. If you want to be able to guarantee that your interactions with other people are not constantly being sidetracked, you need to learn how you can focus.

Stoics emphasizes that we must make it a point to act, not by reaction, but by purposeful action. Make sure that you focus on what you want to do and keep your mind on it. Mindfully focus. Let yourself stay entirely dedicated to what matters in that moment. If you can do so, you will be far more successful than you imagined.

Get Rid of Ego

We regularly find ourselves caught up in believing that ultimately, we are the most important aspects of our lives. We get stuck in this belief that we are what matters the most—and sure, in our own lives, we are the center. However, it is important to recognize that we are not all-important. This is a lesson that empaths, in particular, need to learn. While you may be quick to shrug this one off and say that you are not egotistical, when is the last time that you assumed that you were the root of a problem rather than it being entirely unrelated to you? Have you told yourself that when someone close to you was upset that it was your own fault? That is egotistical.

Remember, you do not know everything. You are not omnipotent. You do not know what is going on in someone else's mind. Let go of the idea that you are more important than you are and remind yourself of the insignificance of each and every one of us. The universe is constantly growing and changing. Things varied greatly now form a year ago. This is normal. However, what is not normal is believing that you are at the heart of it all. Let go of that belief. Move on. Even if you feel bad about something, it is probably not on you.

Write Often

Journaling is powerful for just about anyone—so powerful that we have seen it repeatedly throughout the book. Make sure that you take the time every day to journal. It is good for you. Reflect on the day that you had. Take the time to consider the way in which you responded to someone or something. Remember the truth of the matter—that you can change your own interactions with ease if you know what you are doing. You just have to reflect and learn.

Be Firm

Remember that you should be firm with yourself. Do not back down. Stand your ground. No matter what it is that someone requests of you, remind yourself that you ought to be true to your virtues. Do not forget that ultimately, you owe yourself one thing: Being true to yourself.

It can be difficult in this day and age—especially if you are a woman, you have probably been taught repeatedly that you owe people your help or that you must make yourself likable. However, that is not the case. You owe nothing. You should remember to be firm and true to your values so that you can be successful in your life. Do not let other people drag you down. Do not let the way that other people see you change how you behave. Always do what is right for you without regard to other people—it will help you immensely.

If you know that something is right, stand firm. It will help you avoid letting other people take advantage of you.

Imagine the Worst-Case Scenario

While we have talked about how anxiety is a problem, being able to stop and consider the negativity or worst-case scenario, without letting it hold you back, is a practice in temperance. Remember, you must be able to overcome your fear—that means that fear must be present to some degree.

Inviting that contemplation into what may eventually be the case is a great way for you to stop and consider those fears so that you can learn from them. Take some time to think about what might happen if things go wrong. Then, consider how you can handle those situations and how you can or should change what you do today in anticipation.

Ask yourself what things would look like if things went wrong tomorrow or next week.

Ask yourself how you would cope with that particular situation if it were to arise.

Ask yourself if you need to change your life today to cope with tomorrow.

The truth is, you do not have to change today for tomorrow, and even if things go wrong tomorrow, could you really have changed them in the first place? This teaches you resilience and tolerance—both of which matter immensely.

Accept That Nothing Lasts Forever

Finally, remind yourself that nothing in life is forever. Everything will die at some point. The sun will stop shining. The earth will disappear. This is only natural—things age, decay, and die. And ultimately, nothing that you do today will change that. Nothing that you do can prevent that ultimate ending, which means that you need to think accordingly. You need to plan accordingly. You must make sure that what you do in life will bring you joy today. This means that you do not have to let yourself be used by other people—in the grand scheme of things, it is worthless and futile to even bother. You do not have to chase accomplishments hoping to do something grand—no one will remember it. Live your life on your own terms. Live a life that you enjoy. That is the only way to live a good, true life, according to the Stoics, and that is entirely applicable to the empath as well.

Conclusion

Thank you for making it through to the end of *Stoicism And The Art Of Happiness*. Hopefully, you found this book and everything within it to be highly beneficial to you as you read it! As you read, you were introduced to a wide range of topics designed to benefit you. From being able to recognize the truth all around you to be able to see how empaths can absorb too much emotions and how to prevent it, this book was meant to provide you with information that you could use to live your best life out in a world where nothing lasts forever. You deserve to live a life that you can enjoy, no matter what kind of life that is.

Remember, ultimately, being able to live stoically is highly beneficial to the empath. Being a Stoic empath is just one way that you can make sure that you defend yourself and your mind from the anxiety and stress that can come with the constant inundation of emotions that are common. With the Stoic mindset, you can remind yourself what really matters. You can learn to live a life led by logic and reason instead of constantly being exposed to your emotions. All you have to do is take the time to apply it.

The next step for you is to get started Start using some of those tools that were provided so that you can successfully change the way that you treat those around you. Make sure that you are constantly working to better yourself and the control that you have over yourself so that you are able to succeed in minding your emotions and living a successful life. It does not take much to begin living life Stoically, and the benefits that it can bring can be life-changing if you can learn how to utilize them accordingly.

Thank you for taking the time to reach the end of this book. As you read, hopefully, you learned something new that you can begin to apply to your own life! Hopefully, you are feeling more empowered now than ever, and like you can take back the control over your life once and for all. Good luck as you dive deeper into these different states of mind so that you can begin to live the life that you want to lead. Thank you once more, and please, if you found that this book was beneficial to you in any way or helped you out, head over to Amazon to leave a quick review! Support from the readers is always greatly appreciated and highly recommended!

Printed in Great Britain
by Amazon